Flights of Fancy

Flights of Fancy

The Love Letters of Margaret McLaren-Reid

as reconstructed by

Richard Cullen

Published 2025 in Great Britain and the USA by
EnvelopeBooks

12 Wellfield Avenue, London N10 2EA
116 West 73rd Street, New York, NY 10023

© Richard Cullen

Richard Cullen asserts his right to be identified as the Author of the Work, and Editor of the quoted correspondence, in accordance with the Copyright, Designs and Patents Act 1988

Stephen Games asserts his right to be identified as the Editor of the Work in accordance with the Copyright, Designs and Patents Act 1988

All rights reserved. No part of this book may be reproduced, stored or transmitted in any form or by any means, mechanical or electronic, including photocopying and recording, or by any information storage or retrieval system, without the written permission of Envelope Books, nor be otherwise circulated in any form of binding or cover other than that in which it is published and without a similar condition being imposed on the subsequent purchaser.

A CIP catalogue record is available from the British Library

Cover and interior designed by Stephen Games | Booklaunch
Cover photo: 1931 Hawker Fury Mk 1 | Malcolm Haines, Alamy

EnvelopeBooks 32
ISBN 9781915023612
www.envelopebooks.co.uk

For Moniek

TELEPHONE
2020 HOVE.
AT HOME 2 TO 3 P.M.
EXCEPT SATURDAYS.

17, BRUNSWICK SQUARE,
HOVE,
SUSSEX.

10 Feb. 1922.

Dearest Peggy,

Though I have not written to you, I have been thinking ever so much about you since you deserted the "old post-box" for doing his father to take up with a strange man! I am always most anxious to hear your letters read out. I am much relieved to find that up to date anyhow the

Contents

Foreword	1
Introduction	3
The families	7
1. Tell our story	9
2. Begin at the beginning	15
3. Mespot	29
4. Motherhood and misery	39
5. Harry in Kurdistan	47
6. Young widow	59
7. Life begins to return	67
8. Rivals: Harry vs Bonzo	73
Harry in the Doldrums	83
Harry in Italy	90
9. The Big Leap	99
10. Married life—and other adjustments	109
11. Frontier days	123
Me—in Quetta!	125
12. To Chile	143
13. Wartime tussles	159
14. Alarms at Home	173
15. Marking time—the war, Part 3	195
16. Final fling?	201
Mediterranean mayhem	201
Bulgaria	213
17. Fading away …	221
18. Aftermath—as reported	231

Continued overleaf

Appendix	237
Harry Reid—step by step through an RAF career	237
Honours and Mentions	239
Special qualifications	239
Acknowledgements	241
Abbreviations	243
Bibliography	245
Publications	245
Internet	246
Newspapers	247
Illustration and quotation credits	248

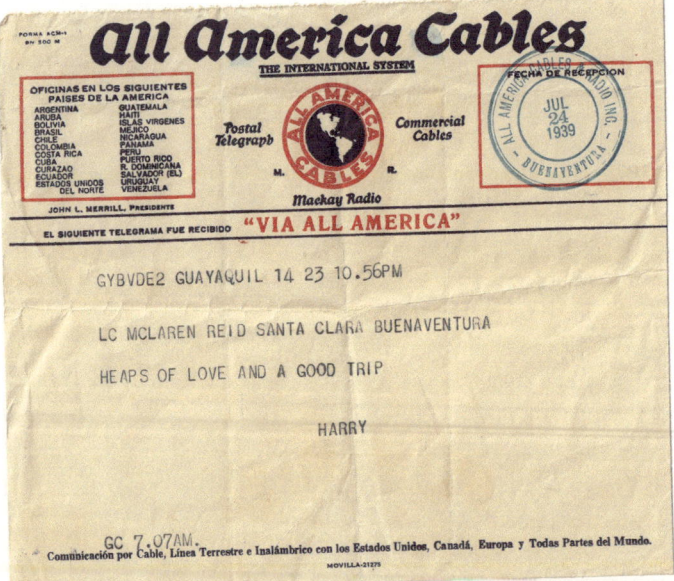

Foreword
by Air Commodore Graham R. Pitchfork
M.B.E., B.A., F.R.Ae.S.

The human story behind a group of medals can provide a fascinating insight into bygone activities, social behaviour and history. All and many others are encapsulated in this account.

The novel approach adopted by the author takes the reader through a unique period of British and colonial history, as seen through the eyes and words of two people who were devoted to each other. Their life during the decades that followed the First World War reminds us of a life that was routine and accepted by service families all those years ago. Long periods of separation, travel and adventure to various exotic places, risks taken in their stride and all at a time when letters, some taking weeks, were the only means of staying in contact. Through all this, the relationship between Harry and Margaret, and the love they shared, held firm.

In addition to what it says about the main characters, the book reminds the reader of an epoch in the history of the RAF when 'air policing' became a feature of dealing with troublesome tribes in areas controlled by the British. The dangers of such flying in the remote regions of Iraq and the Indian North-West Frontier are graphically described, but against the backdrop of the unique lifestyle that went along with such appointments. We learn also about service as a diplomat in South America, an aspect of RAF operations about which little is known.

As one might expect, there are some downsides to lives

lived in such circumstances and the author reminds us of the difficulties experienced by young children who necessarily spend a great deal of their time separated from their parents.

But the underlying theme of the book is one of deep affection and a determination to combat difficulties in order to be together, set against the backdrop of a fascinating period in British military and social history, the likes of which we will not experience again.

Graham Pitchfork
Gloucestershire 2025

Introduction
by Richard Cullen
Editor

Ah, Serendipity![1] You do pick your moments ... Yes, I expected the letters but I didn't expect to be blown over by them. They, and then Cat and her father, pushed me past the point of no return, but I would never have met Cat without the intervention of a very helpful auctioneer and an agreement I made with her. So I certainly got more than I bargained for.

Many years ago I bought some miniature medals at auction. As part of the arrangement, I agreed to take a battered cool box jammed with some 740 handwritten letters dating from the early 1920s and some photographs relating to a decorated RAF pilot. Of the letters, 450 were from the pilot to his wife, with the rest being to her from her parents and son. There were also some books. All told, they revealed an intriguing love affair, exciting travel, family trauma and a fascinating insight into the times.

My main interest had been the medals, but it did not take me long to realise that this collection of photographs, books and old letters was the *real* treasure.

I should explain. 'Cat' is Catriona Newington, the great niece of Margaret McLaren-Reid, the recipient of all the letters sent by Harry, her husband, whose medals I had bought. Through those letters, Cat introduced me to her parents, their

---

[1] Serendipity: 'the fact of finding interesting or valuable things by chance'. *Cambridge Dictionary*

own recollections of the couple and a wealth of family ephemera and photographs. Among them, winking at me, was an image of Margaret (*above*)—almost a century old. And, like many before me, I was entranced ...

As I delved further into the letters I uncovered very much more than an extraordinary romance: there were adventures in Arabia, India and South America; high living; family strife;

unusual goings on during the Second World War; and endless uncertainty. Here was a story that I felt impelled to tell.

But I had a problem. The information flow was all one-way —*to* Margaret. I had nothing *from* her. So, while the service career and correspondence of Harry (*above*) are available to us, the sweet nothings that doubtlessly greeted *his* ear remain silent. I decided to invent them.

Telling the story from *her* perspective meant this had to be *their* story, not just a Harry biography (which is how it began). I had to intersperse quotations from letters to her and add background information that shed light on the circumstances in which both Harry and Margaret lived: a dance between fiction and non-fiction.

Nevertheless, save very occasional embellishment to fill in gaps, the story is a true one. It begins in the aftermath of the First World War, in Iraq, where Britain was struggling to administer a fledgling country carved out of the Ottoman Empire. A hundred years ago, Harry fought there against the Kurdish peoples; Margaret lived among them. Since then, British servicemen have returned to fight and die in two wars and a failed attempt at peacekeeping. The region is still in turmoil and the Kurds are still stateless.

Harry's language, which you will gather from his letters, would label him today as vain, chauvinistic and arrogant. While some of his observations about women are outrageous, I hope that we manage to reflect that his behaviour, attitudes and language are of another age, far different from anything we would endorse today.

Except for the books that help set the scene, all quotations are from letters sent to Margaret by Harry, and by her father, mother and son Alasdair, together with the dates they were written.

And they really are verbatim.

The families

Margaret McLaren-Reid, née Copeman
Arthur Copeman—Margaret's father
Eva Copeman (née Wilkin)—Margaret's mother
Angela Whittome (née Copeman)—Margaret's sister
Vice Admiral Sir Nicholas Copeman, D.S.C.—Margaret's brother
Michael Copeman—Margaret's brother

Group Captain Harry McLaren-Reid, D.F.C.—Margaret's second husband
Alasdair McLaren-Reid—their son (Margaret's second)
Alice Reid, née McLaren—Harry's mother
Claude McLaren Reid, 'Toby'—Harry's brother
Sylvia McLaren Davis, née Reid—Harry's sister

Lieutenant Colonel Horace Goldsmith, M.C.—Margaret's first husband
David Goldsmith—Horace and Margaret's son
Major General George Fanshawe, C.B., D.S.O., 'Bonzo'— Margaret's suitor, who was later briefly engaged to Angela
Sir Maurice Whittome—Angela's husband
Violet Copeman (née King), 'Bunty'—Nicholas's wife
Barbara Copeman (née Odling)—Michael's wife
Irene Reid 'Bunny' (née Hall-Dalwood)—Claude's wife
Alan Davis—Sylvia's husband

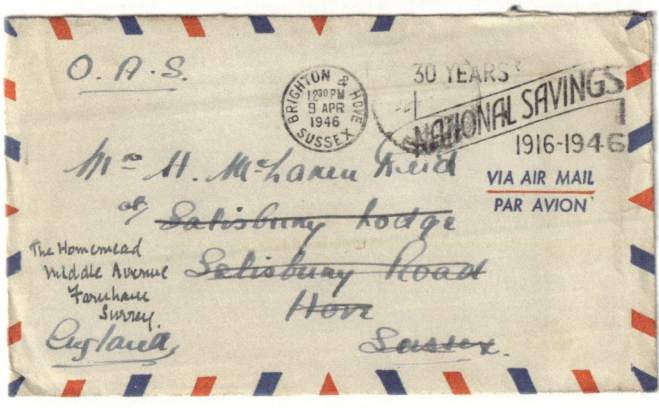

Chapter 1
Tell our story

> Our friends drank your health to the tune of
> 50 bottles of bubbly.
> DADDY TO ME, 4 OCTOBER 1927

Bodies. Funny things. Mine is well past its former glory. 'Vain,' do you say? Yes, but others will agree with me: something of a siren but surprisingly monogamous, despite various temptations along the way. That doesn't mean I didn't flirt. I was good at that—maybe *too* good, if you ask those who fought over me or tried to lead me astray. And perhaps I missed out. Well, it's a bit late now to query what I did or didn't do when I was younger. But sometimes I quietly wonder … .

But I have gone off track already. If I am to open my memory box properly, I should perhaps concentrate on my two sons—those bodies that I brought into this world. I miss one and failed the other and I rack my brains trying to understand where I went wrong. Did I really think I had the boy's best interests at heart, however misguided, or was I simply selfish in putting my husband, and our life together, before his needs? And am I ready to wrestle with this?

What is all this about, then? Well, my name is Margaret Eva Heathcote McLaren-Reid. As my author and editor, Richard Cullen, imagines me writing this, it is 1975, I am the same age as the century and I have only four more years to live. I am not very well and am stretching out my days in the wilds of Wiltshire with Harry, my beautiful and wonderful husband. And, while I'm surrounded by drawers full of silk knickers, too many fur coats and endless empty scent bottles to remind me of more exuberant days, my body is still alive. Hugs, caresses and Harry's kisses keep it fed.

This is his fault. He wallows in nostalgia and thinks I should tell our story. What the hell for? It's old hat. We had a lot of fun and adventure. And that's it. It's over.

But I have given in to the old charmer. To make life easier he has rigged up a rather clever recording gadget that switches on when I think of something to say but goes to sleep when I falter into silence—which I expect will happen a lot. He promises he will mix me the occasional stiffener as a reward for progress. Expect a lot of staccato.

Where to start? Well, I suppose I *was* a little naughty. I was dishy, the war was over and everyone danced and partied endlessly. Why ever not? And I did run away for my first husband. Which left Alasdair—my second son; not our crowning achievement perhaps. Dare I explain?

But wasn't it the King in *Alice's Adventures in Wonderland* who told the White Rabbit to 'Begin at the beginning ... and go on until you come to the end: then stop.' I won't do this just yet. I think I'll start instead at the point when Harry finally got me over the line. After ten months of his asking, I finally relented in November 1926 and nearly a year later, on 1 October 1927, we were married at Hove, not far from the parental pile. And what a bang it was. At last the family got what I had rejected five long years before: a grand party, admired by all and heaps of happy fun, despite some dismal weather.

Everybody came. We all crammed into St Andrew's Church and drowned in vicars—there were three. My uncle Gary did the nuptial stuff, the local bishop gave a thumping address and the resident cleric read the prayers. *This time* Daddy was there to give me away.

Harry and I looked magnificent. What with my little David running around, I could hardly call myself *virgo intacta*, so white was out of the question—*ergo* I wore gold lamé and lace. I can

Harry and I on our wedding day: 1 October 1927.

see it now: gown sweeping down to the floor just covering T-strapped satin shoes with heels that took me a couple of inches off the floor and closer to Harry's great height; golden bandeau on my hair fixed with Mama's diamond pin, pearls around my neck and Harry's beautiful diamond brooch sparkling just below. I carried a shower bouquet of deep red carnations and a feathery fern. Perfect. I stunned them all.

Harry and his best man were resplendent in RAF full-dress complete with medals. I was very proud. I had two maids of honour—sister Angela and cousin Bunny—whose taffeta dresses provided the 'blue' element to the proceedings: yet more colour to add to all the other flowers (thank you, Mama). So you will understand why I was rather miffed when the local paper reported that it was the music for which the occasion would be remembered.

Talk about a cast of thousands: Copemans and Wilkinses, aunts, uncles, cousins and siblings, all together for the first time in ages. Harry's fellow officers were there in force along with an illustrious selection of family friends and Daddy's business cronies from Brighton, Hove and wider Sussex. Add in several friends from London and we conjured up the social event of the year. Everyone in their best bib and tucker: even Grandmama had dug out her finery and jewels. Such a pity that Harry's family was nowhere to be seen.[1]

We also had the Navy (brother Nick) and the Army (Bonzo *et al*) and together with the RAF contingent they ushered us out of the church beneath crossed swords. My, they were good-looking: rich pickings for Angela, I thought at the time. In fact, in spite of the swathe of gallant military men, Angela eventually went on to marry Maurice Whittome, one of the guests but very much a civilian.

---

[1] Brother Toby was working in Malaya; sister Sylvia was working in Florence as well as watching over Mother Alice, and Aunt Bessie was at home in Scotland.

We all hived off along the sea front to the Bedford Hotel where Daddy and Mama welcomed everyone to what became a tremendous party with 130 guests or so. They had decked the place out with flowers, installed the small band that the local paper had raved about, and laid on plenty to eat and drink, so nothing could possibly go wrong. Everyone spoiled David who, at just five years old, did his best to steal the show; and to my great relief (and surprise) John Hawtrey, Harry's best man, managed to stick to gentle ribbing and steer clear of the type of jokes that would normally abound during mealtimes in the mess, in spite of the quantities of Champagne we had all downed.

Having cut the cake with Harry's sword and paid final *salaams* to the guests, Harry and I changed and, showered with rose petals, left them all to it. We jumped on a train and steamed up to London where we made a beeline for the Rubens.[2] There, fuelled with oysters and yet more Champagne, I let Harry off the leash. And my, was he keen to make up for lost time. I didn't complain … . Well, the poor lamb had been very patient (and come to think of it, so had I).

In the morning, having feasted on coffee, smoked salmon and scrambled eggs, we cabbed to Victoria and jumped on a train which took us to Dover. After a rather choppy crossing to Calais we proceeded to Paris where we boarded the Simplon Orient Express, which carried us on to Venice in great style—very glam. In fact, holed up in our hotel, we didn't see much of Venice and resolved to return. Then, on to Florence and our honeymoon; but more of that later.

Meanwhile, the aged relatives basked in their triumph and shifted to Hove's Regency Hotel where Mama swept up waifs and strays for dinner and Daddy (wallowing in his recent retirement) was astounded at the continuing consumption and ever-increasing cost of the Champagne. Harry and I later

---

[2] The Rubens Hotel in Buckingham Palace Road.

learned that little David had consumed all kinds of goodies without apparent mishap (including some fizz). Bonzo drove him home where he flaked out, and then joined Angela at the Metropole, where the younger bucks set about keeping the show alive until the small hours.

Mama of course made sure that the local press was fully briefed on the whole event, including a list of the deluge of presents. Daddy was 'somewhat annoyed' when he found out that Harry's best man and a couple of friends had hived off to their bedroom and ordered three more bottles of Champagne, which added to his grumbles when the bills started coming in.

But all was forgotten by the time they retired to their huge home back in Hove.

Mama wallowed in the praise that followed, being congratulated from all directions for the 'beauty', 'luxury', 'liveliness' and 'style' of the event. And Grandmama declared the whole thing a 'huge and social success', which more than made up for the disappointment I had heaped on the family when I ran off and married Horace.[3]

[3] Horace Goldsmith q.v.

Chapter 2
Begin at the beginning

*Since you deserted your doting old father
to take up with a strange man …*
DADDY TO ME, 10 FEBRUARY 1922

I was born on 6 October 1900 at Cowes on the Isle of Wight. I remember little about it but Mama was never slow to remind me that rather than sail into the world, I took my time, which she found very painful. Still, that didn't stop her from producing three more: another girl and two boys. Daddy—Alfred Copeman—was a rather distinguished surgeon.

Mama—Eva Florence—was the daughter of Sir Walter Wilkin, who was a big-shot barrister in London. KCMG (Kindly Call Me God) and all that. He became Lord Mayor of London and knew Queen Victoria.[1] Mama liked the social merry-go-round. She was very well connected and famous for her lavish parties and dances, particularly those in the run-up to Christmas.

Daddy came from an old Norfolk family, was Cambridge-

---

[1] Sir Walter Henry, K.C.M.G., b. 1842; ed. Brentwood and City of London Sch.; Bar. Middle Temple 1875; formerly Lieut.-Col. and Hon. Col. 3rd Middlesex Artillery Vol. (VD); Sheriff of London 1892–3 and Lord Mayor of London 1895–6; Alderman of London (Lime Street Ward) from 1888; J.P. and a Lieut. of City of London; Knight of several Foreign Orders:, K.C.M.G. 1896. 43, Gloucester Square, Hyde Park, W.
https://www.genealogy.com/forum/surnames/topics/wilkin/310/
Accessed 10 Nov 2020

educated and became a member of the Commission of Lieutenancy for the City of London. Very fancy. He was also very religious, maybe not surprisingly as his father was a vicar. He famously survived a shipwreck off Australia in 1895 while gadding around the world. He was also mad on sports—particularly golf, yachts and fishing.

Mama married Daddy in December 1899 so my appearance was just decent. Sister Angela arrived just over a year later, followed by brothers Nick when I was six and Michael two years after that.

We had a comfy childhood. Lovely clothes, huge house, plenty of servants—all the trappings. Home was a Georgian townhouse in Pavilion Parade in Brighton: five storeys above ground, I think. The servants inhabited the top two floors and the basement with its huge kitchen and everything ran like clockwork. What with Daddy's medical and business partners, Mama's various ladies' activities, endless bridge parties and guests from London, the house was always full. Of course, the war dampened all that somewhat, but it did wonders for us women and our sense of freedom.

I spent the whole of the war at school in Gloucester. Nothing much to report here. I did all right, was good at games and had time to think. Rations were a bit thin at times and I learned how to grow vegetables. I was a keen Girl Guide. I loved books and not just novels: I read about travel and art. One of my friends steered me towards Kipling and India.

While we tried hard not to think about the war, many of my friends lost brothers and fathers in France. I was lucky because Daddy worked in Brighton throughout the war and because our fates were random, it was not something we talked about.

Everybody knows about the Royal Pavilion: that fanciful monument to George IV (they say 'playground') with all its rounded domes, minarets and facades. Well, the war gave it a purpose and this imitation Eastern palace became a real one when adapted as a hospital for Indians wounded in France and Belgium. We saw it all: it was right opposite our house. I was fascinated. Strange people I later learned to be Pathans, Sikhs, Gurkhas, Mahrattas, Bengalis and others appeared. As if by magic, the palace opened up to them, although most of course

Eva Copeman holding Angela, with me on the floor. Early 1904.

The Brighton Pavilion being used as a hospital for Indian soldiers, 1915.

were inside being treated. But those who were recovering were allowed out into the gardens and we could see them in their blue hospital uniforms. Doctor Daddy was delighted by the pavilion's new function: he was chummy with Colonel Coats, the old India hand who ran the hospital.[2] In 1916 the Indians left France to fight in the Middle East and the hospital switched to caring for those who had lost limbs. Still, the blue uniforms carried on.

There were those who objected to all these carryings on, including Mama, who had been rather dubious about them from the start. But then Mama had very firm opinions. She

---

[2] Colonel George Coats C.B. was a retired Indian Army soldier who presided over a committee of representatives which was formed in 1915 to approve the arrangements made for the Indians. Patients were grouped in the different wards according to their caste and were provided with Indian attendants of similar castes to care for them.
http://www.sikhmuseum.com/brighton/doctor/pavilion/caste.html
Accessed 23 July, 2021.

could be very superior—she thought that Brighton was being taken over by vulgar *nouveau riche* types who, in her opinion, were spoiling the town's reputation by introducing what she would call 'bad taste' to its growth and entertainments. I'm sure that today she would be dismissed as an outrageous snob. And as for the thought of me or anyone of my 'breeding' doing anything related to employment:—unimaginable. Doing 'good work' was only alright if word about it reached the right ears.

I only witnessed the comings and goings at the Pavilion during the holidays but I was fascinated. Those magnificent Sikhs! I wanted to help out there but Mama stamped on that; it was 'not suitable for a young lady' (meaning she feared I would not be safe). Our school did however let me and other Guides help at a convalescent home near Tewksbury, but that was only for officers.

At the same time, Mama had her fingers in all sorts of voluntary pies. I remember she worked very hard to raise money and organise support for refugees from Belgium and other displaced persons. In that sense, she was full of contradictions. But as for *me* getting too near to the Indians: No.

Then—Armistice Day, 1918. The war was over at last. I was barely eighteen years old and had everything to play for, although it would be another ten years before I could vote. For some reason or none at all, our family had emerged unscathed. At home, however, although freedom may have been in the air, Angela and I hardly felt it. We hated Mama's insistence on being escorted everywhere. Sometimes it felt as though I couldn't brush my teeth without a chaperone breathing down my neck.

The war changed things, though. Not long after it was over, the family moved from Brighton to 17 Brunswick Square in neighbouring Hove, another enormous Regency Era pile alongside a long green expanse full of trees and tennis courts, but with a tiny garden. A much-feted British painter had been born there and that somehow set the scene.[3] By now there were fewer of us at home. In spite of Mama's prejudices, Angela was now up in London and learning to be a kindergarten teacher, Nick was at Osborne Naval College on the Isle of Wight and Mike was boarding at a prep school not far away. That just left me, my parents and (I think) the four women who looked after us. As far as I could see, their only plan was to get me married off and I didn't like it, nor all the parental expectation that went with marriage. And of course, the choice was very limited, with so many young men having been killed or maimed during the hostilities.

Whether or not it was part of a plot to 'advertise me', Daddy had arranged for a chap called Horne to photograph me as a seventeenth birthday present (*see page 4*). The effect of this photograph, taken when I was still sixteen, was to catapult at least three men in my direction, and I was rather choosy about who I dished it out to. (And would you believe, both Angela's sons still give that photograph pride of place in their homes, to the continued ire of their wives.)

Well, the first to fall was Horace Goldsmith.[4] He was a soldier: tall, brave and dashing. I met him at a convalescent home in Llangammarch Wells in Wales in 1919; our family was relaxing at a big country hotel and he was in a hospital for officers nearby.

---

[3] Robert Polehill Bevan 1865–1925.

[4] Horace Armstrong Goldsmith. Born in 1886 in Central India. Commissioned in the East Yorkshire Regiment in 1905. Transferred to 95th Russell's Infantry at Calcutta in 1912. Served in Mesopotamia 1914–16, earning a Military Cross at Kut al Mara. After UK leave 1917–19 (Lt. Col.), appointed Political Officer at Sulaymaniyah, Iraq in 1920. Tall, handsome and described variously by his peers as 'a delightful fellow' and 'a mild-tempered student-like type'. 'Believed that bombing was the only way to impose civilisation on the tribes in the region he administered.'

We grew close. I liked him because he was kind, funny and, for a soldier, unstuffy. Unlike other chinless wonders dangled in my direction, he was worldly. And he was crazy about me.

Daddy did not take to him. He thought 'Goldsmith' wasn't 'quite right'. Mama, however, saw that there were limits to which she could push a rebellious daughter and decided that he would just about 'do'. To add to Daddy's dismay, she allowed Angela and me to holiday in Montana-sur-Sierre in Switzerland

Horace with me in the snow at Montana-sur-Sierre, 1920.

the following February, with Horace and a group of friends. By the time we returned he had asked me to marry him and I had said 'Yes'. Despite much reluctance, my parents were decent enough to announce our engagement on 9 June 1920. I was 19.

Horace had been in Mesopotamia during the war and was now preparing to return there to work with the Iraq Civil Administration. It took some time for the authorities to decide what his role should be and where he would be based, but by the end of the year he was writing to me from a town called Sulaimania (*now Sulaymaniyah*). This would become my home.

Luckily, a return to Llangammarch Wells in August with him and my parents helped to thaw the ice somewhat and there began what you might call an uneasy peace. Horace's sister Bella, whom I now met for the first time, won prizes for managing to soothe the parental disquiet.

The year 1921 came and went. I learned to be a good correspondent and our letters kept me going. Horace sent me photographs of Sulaimania which, while intriguing me, filled my parents with horror: they really struggled to think why on Earth I would want to go and live there.

Horace's bungalow at Sulaimania, 1921. My surprisingly nice new home!

Otherwise we all pretended that everything was normal. We had a lovely holiday in Scotland in August and Nick was able to join us. We stayed at a place called Boat-of-Garten on the River Spey, which was chosen, of course, because of the rich salmon and trout fishing.

While Daddy concentrated on his rod and flies, the rest of us relaxed, rambled and revelled. I remember the ospreys that we saw: beautiful birds.

Time slipped by. We played plenty of tennis and golf and Mama would indulge herself with an occasional escape from Daddy at a quiet hotel somewhere or other. And I kept up my interest in gardening and learned to play bridge (badly, unlike my sister, who just seemed to understand her cards).

Angela by now was beginning to bloom. She was ahead of me in her obsession with style and the current shift to simpler clothes. Clothes had always been a concern of hers (*see page 24*).

> Angela is becoming a model young lady—spends quite a long time on her "look" at home and is much cleaner and tidier.
>
> DADDY TO MARGARET, 6 OCTOBER 1917

She seemed able to keep up with ever-changing fashions and encouraged me to follow the trends. She introduced me to new shapes and materials, and thanks to Daddy's generous allowances we were able to indulge ourselves. Before very long I had caught up with her. And we discovered lipstick.

But for all this there lingered the ever-present ghost. I was going to marry Horace and the family was increasingly bothered by the thought of my rotting in some hot and dusty town in the middle of nowhere. Why did they have so little trust?

Maybe that's what impelled me to run off to meet him at Marseilles when he docked there in the new year.

To her credit, Mama came along too—all the way! She said that she wanted to make sure that I didn't get lost and that we

'Angela is becoming a model young lady.' 6 October 1917.

eloped in style (by Golden Arrow to Dover, *Flèche d'Or* from Calais, then the *Paris-Lyon-Méditerranée* Pullman, which dropped us off at Lyon in time for the final leg to Marseilles). I think the real reason was that she didn't want to miss the party, however small it would be.

Why did I do it? I can't say I remember *deciding* to rebel. But there I was: twenty, tall, pretty and awfully bored by the procession of uninspiring young men whom Mama still hoped might be suitable. All wet behind the ears.

You know, compared with some of the Bold and the Beautiful who flooded the society and scandal pages, I was pretty tame. But now that the family had shifted to the quaint delights of Hove, I wanted some space of my own. Angela and my brothers were younger and they weighed me down. On top of this, there was a new spirit. The war had given women a new slant on life—a kind of independence, the right to work and the wish to enjoy ourselves on our own terms. I could feel it. Fashions became freer. We learned that dancing could (and should) be fun; that *we* could pick who we danced with instead of waiting like cattle for some gormless man to invite us.

That said, decent-looking men were scarce. Horace was *my* choice. He was handsome, delightful and wise and I loved him. He told good stories too.

My last Christmas season in Hove was glorious. Just a few days before my escape, Mama threw one of her big dance parties at the Princes Hotel. Both Angela and I were dressed to the nines. I remember carrying a lovely white plume fan.

Funnily enough, in the event, Mama was terrific at Marseilles, joining in the fun while Daddy fumed and sulked back in Hove; he could not understand what I was doing with that 'strange man' and was fearful that he would ill-treat me.

But at the heart of it all, I think the dear old thing was simply unhappy that Horace had stolen me away. He was typically insistent about what we should and should not do to steer clear of the flu that had struck the south of France, as well as being pessimistic about Britain's future influence in Mesopotamia to which Horace was taking me—and about India too. That was because while Mama took pride in avoiding having any views about politics and foreign affairs, Daddy read avidly and remained a stalwart armchair pundit on such matters for the rest of his life. Much later he confessed he had hoped that the authorities would forbid our marriage in France and that I would return home with my tail between my legs. Knowing also how much my parents scrapped, I suspect that Mama thoroughly enjoyed sending him the cable that announced that permission had been received and our nuptial would take place the following Saturday willy-nilly.

We had wizard fun. We stayed at the Hôtel Splendid, a sumptuous establishment in the centre of the city, in a room that looked straight out to the bay of Marseilles, where we had a wonderful time. We got married of course. The dastardly deed took place on 14 January 1922 at the British Consulate General (*see below*). I was twenty-one, Horace thirty-five. Maybe that was what bothered my father.

Horace and I played and explored each other and drifted east to Cannes for a few days, where we were gorgeously reckless in the Casino Municipal, near Jetée Albert-Édouard. Even in February the place was packed with beautiful, young, free women revelling in their post-war freedom (and with furs everywhere). By the time we left we had also partied and danced in Monaco, Monte Carlo and San Remo, where I felt quite at home. Not bad!

My Marseilles marriage certificate, dated 14 January 1922. Golly!

Envelope containing one of Harry's early letters from Kirkuk.

Iraq, with places referred to in the account of my travels, 1922–24.

Chapter 3
Mespot

> I am much relieved to find that … the strange man is not ill-treating you, unless indeed he has so terrorised you that you dare not complain! Your mother has been working like a Trojan to get all your business done for you. I really think you both owe her a deep debt of gratitude for her manifold efforts.
> DADDY TO ME, 10 FEBRUARY 1922

> The Kurds are a mountain race, with all the characteristics of mountaineers—love of freedom, violent passions and a clannish feeling of pride. These primary traits dispose the Kurd to fly to arms at small provocation and engage with zest in bitter feuds.
> EDWARD NOEL, *THE CHARACTER OF THE KURDS AS ILLUSTRATED BY THEIR PROVERBS AND POPULAR SAYINGS*, 1921

Thinking about this now, I did of course have occasional cold feet about the whole thing. Yes, the thrill of lurching into the unknown with a rather dashing older man did a pretty good job of masking my inner fears and the acknowledgement that it was all a bit reckless. But the truth is, I had almost no idea of what lay in store.

Daddy, dear caring Daddy, had not helped by reminding me about the situation in Mesopotamia and that barely three years had passed since the Kurds rebelled against British rule in the area around where we would be living. He did his best to explain it to me, telling me the history of those ancient and fertile lands that lay within the Tigris–Euphrates river system that had been ruled by the Ottomans for over 400 years and were now divided up between Britain and France.

Iraq—or Irak—the new state to which I was heading—was now mandated to the British and peopled by tribes of bewildering ethnic and religious habit who were difficult to control, notably the Kurds who dreamed of Kurdistan as a permanent land for their people. There were banana skins all over the ground. During the war, Horace had helped to drive the Turks out of Mesopotamia; now he was on his way to be part of the governing effort, but he was also heading into a tribal hotspot—with me in tow.

At some point we left the riviera and sailed off to our destination. Typically, Daddy thought we should have gone on a far fancier ship—well, he would. We passed Gibraltar, went through the Suez Canal, skirted Aden and then sailed on to Bombay—a whole month at sea. It was old hat to Horace of course, but my excitement grew and grew with every landfall we made at the ports along the way.

After a tantalisingly short stay in Bombay, we boarded a ship that went to the Iraqi port at Basra, from where we took a train to Baghdad. 'Took a train' sounds rather grand, does it not? Well, it wasn't: 'First Class' changed its spots. The train carried us overnight to Amara, where a fast boat up the Tigris brought us to Kut, a day-long journey. From Kut we journeyed to Baghdad in another overnight train: two days to travel a mere 350 miles, the equivalent of Brighton to Newcastle. Moments of excitement on the river reduced the tedium but, after a while, even Horace's tales of his antics during the siege of Kut and elsewhere in the region failed to dispel my ennui.

He, of course, was an old India hand so torrential rain, heat and dust were par for the course for him; but for me, despite Horace's encouragement, it was not an enthralling start. The snail's pace at which we travelled was partly caused by flooding along the Euphrates and Tigris rivers, and we arrived at Baghdad to find water everywhere, even though the floods were beginning to retreat.

Horace showed me off with great pride during the short time we spent while in Baghdad and I was excited and thankful to find myself well up to the airs and graces expected of me when first encountering the British community and its 'isms'. I was thankful also that I had enough appropriate clothing—hats and all! Before we set off for Sulaimania and once the floods had waned, Horace took me to see some of his old haunts south of Baghdad around the Tigris. Gosh—to be in the heart of ancient Mesopotamia!

We visited the ancient ruins at Ctesiphon, along with Borsippa, and Babylon—the two big sites around Hilla. It was all completely new to me, quite fascinating and, he told me, very 'Arab'. There was real magic about it all. It became a beautiful spring.

Once we had moved into Horace's house in Sulaimania, I think I adapted well (even taking scorpions in my stride). Some things didn't change; having dropped our cards at all the right households, invitations to tea followed, and eventually to dinner, and I had no objection to becoming a 'memsahib'.

Fortunately we arrived well after the winter snows and the floods that followed had gone, leaving time to prepare for the heat and discomfort of summer. In short, it got bloody hot.

Gradually the furore at Hove began to die down. Mama did a sterling job tidying up the mess that I had left behind and people began to accept that I really was married, even if the circumstances were hardly what the family would have preferred (elopement not quite being Copeman style). They even put an announcement in the local paper to the effect that we had married in the south of France because Horace was recovering from malignant malaria and couldn't risk the cold English climate: utter rubbish!

Wedding at the Residency, Baghdad. March 1922.

To everyone's surprise, I took to my new home rather well and pretty quickly realised I was pregnant (and that I rather liked the process of getting there). To begin, this didn't much get in the way and I was able to explore.

Sulaimania sits in a valley around 2,750 feet high and is almost completely surrounded by mountains, some of which tower some 10,000 feet over the 10,000 or so inhabitants. The ancient history of the region and the tales of the Arab and

Kurdish peoples were fascinating and I really enjoyed my visits to the old town and its bazaars; I even became a dab hand at bargaining. Occasional visits to Baghdad provided variety and reminders of fancier European styles.

At first glance the town itself was rather scruffy and much was in ruins. But once past the crumbling mud walls, there were some sizeable houses built with burnt brick that I was told resembled houses in Persia (the border of which we were quite near). We lived in one of these. It had a pretty garden and veranda and we were very comfortable.

Perhaps I should not have been surprised, but at the back of it all there was an unspoken understanding about our having to 'keep the show together'. We may have been in the middle of nowhere, but were expected to behave as formally as we would have done back in England. That meant that we dressed as if we were off to Ascot and ate with our best silver. Thankfully life at Sulaimania was a little less starchy, but in Baghdad ... oh!

Horace's main job was to maintain some kind of law and order among the various Kurdish tribes in the hills, while keeping an eye on Turkish attempts to stir up trouble from across the border to the North, and coping with wild tribesmen in Persia to the East. His patch (or *liwa*) contained a population of over 220,000, almost all of whom were Kurds, and his work required a fair bit of travel and endless meetings with the tribes and their rulers. He was good at this—and while the Kurds differed from the Arabs, with whom he had worked so closely in the war, he learned fast and got on well with all of them, including the wildest of the tribesmen, who respected him despite, or perhaps because of, his administrative toughness.

He took me on a couple of his inspection trips, notably to Halabja, where we met the redoubtable Lady Adila, the ruler of the Jaf tribe: now *she* carried some clout. The British called her 'The Princess of the Brave'.

We needed to be brave too. The countryside was rugged and the roads were a trial for Horace's old 'Tin-Lizzie' Ford.

The road from Baghdad was paved but that was about that.

But the Kurds: for me they were the real fascination. In the town they were industrious, busy with bazaars and trading tobacco. Labourers scurried around with wood and produce of all kinds. There were heaps of seasonal fruits and Heaven knows what else, and the people seemed prosperous. In the country, however, the people lived hard lives. In their tents, at night, they had little protection when the *reshabar* —the 'black wind' of Kurdistan—blew up. It was hot and relaxing in the summer and bitterly cold in winter. In the winter they grew wheat and barley, followed by maize, millet and lentils in the summer and—where there was water—rice. The nomadic tribes provided sheep and goats. And the women worked just as hard as the men (although you could hardly say that's unusual).

One thing I should say about the men is that they sported an extraordinary range of head dress—wound this way, tied that way, with every material under the sun. They had terrific style. They also liked to dance … .

There was just one fly in the ointment, which of course I should have foreseen. Compared with all the gaiety to be had in post-war England, there was not a lot of fun out here in Iraq—especially not for a lively twenty-two-year-old—and I don't think poor Horace, fourteen years older than me, understood what I was missing. Or maybe he did, because it was he who introduced me to Harry.

Nevertheless Horace was proud of me. I stood head and shoulders above the other foreign women—literally and, if I may say so, metaphorically. But I didn't stray. Mild flirtations maybe, but nothing physical. I was happy. We both were.

As political officer, Horace was responsible for the Britons in Sulaimania, including visiting military. He would meet visiting RAF aircrew and we often put them up for a day or two.

One day a young officer called Harry Reid flew in from Baghdad and Horace brought him and his observer home for

Kurdish women at a well.

tea—a chap called Nicholson. What a pair. They regaled us with their tales of shooting buzzards and hunting gazelles, and the odd forced landing in the desert. It was obvious that they enjoyed a spot of mischief, and they hadn't managed to clean up very well, which left us thinking that flying must be a pretty grubby and smelly exercise.

Harry was like a boy; physically gorgeous, unbelievably tall and bursting with energy and charm: impossible not to notice.

Harry McLaren-Reid with his father, also a Harry, and sister Sylvia.

Very slowly I built a picture of him and his origins, little of which was what you would describe as 'standard'.

He was born at his mother's family home in Scotland on 23 December, 1899, while she was visiting her parents. She was Alice and her maiden name was 'McLaren' and McLaren became the third of Harry's Christian names—after 'Redvers' (the origins of which I am still not sure of). Having given birth, Alice returned with Harry to Argentina, to re-join her husband Harry Reid, who was a successful rancher. Two siblings followed: Claude in 1902 and Sylvia in 1908.

Harry was brought up gaucho-style. He rode, caught fish and learned to shoot, managed to pick up rudimentary Spanish and developed a deep and lifelong affection for animals. Education was not at that stage a priority.

At some point, however, his parents decided that this had to change. They left their farm behind and returned to England around 1910, settling in Eastbourne, where the parents lived rather grandly for a while while packing off Harry and Claude (who somehow became 'Toby') to a prep school in the town.

The family then moved to Bayswater and in January 1914 Harry moved to Harrow School, where he remained for a couple of years. He told hilarious tales about the place, behaving as some sort of wild colonial boy. I don't think he was any great shakes academically but he was crazy about fitness and sport, especially football and running. His youthful prowess didn't save him from knockouts in the boxing ring but he loved boxing and in later years managed to persuade the RAF that he would make a useful boxing instructor.

Harry never revealed to me why he left school so early. His father had died in 1917 and perhaps the family fortune was insufficient to maintain the mother's lifestyle and the children's schooling. Whatever the case, he signed on with the Royal Naval Air Service at Greenwich in March 1918 aged eighteen, transferred to the fledgling Royal Air Force, and made his first flight after three months. He went solo eleven days later and, exceptionally, went on to become a flying instructor early in 1919.

Not long after, hundreds of servicemen found themselves surplus to requirements following the end of the war. Harry was one of them—still, his flying skills were remembered and he was recalled in May 1921. The following January he was on his way to Iraq where he joined No. 6 Squadron. I met him at the end of that year. He was twenty-two.

Chapter 4
Motherhood and misery

> His successor, Goldsmith, a delightful fellow who had done well in the south and in Khanaquin, was in poor health. The atmosphere I found on arrival [early in 1922] was what would have been described in the jargon of a later period as 'distinctly jittery'. The APO [Assistant Political Officer] I was to relieve at Halabja was on the verge of a nervous breakdown.
> CECIL EDMUNDS, *KURDS, TURKS AND ARABS*, OUP 1957

My recollections of Sulaimania may all sound rather cosy, but far from it. Horace had returned to duty just in time to catch the rumblings of dissent and anti-British fervour among the Kurds. These swelled among the tribes in his district, and one of his colleagues at Ranya, a town about 100 miles north of us, had alarming information about Turkish mischief in Rowanduz district, where more militant Kurds were calling for an independent Kurdistan.[5] For a while, a low-level army intervention combined with RAF bombing raids kept this disquiet under some sort of control.

Horace and his colleagues monitored these threatening influences closely. We had barely settled into life at Sulaimania

---

[5] The Kurds are one of various indigenous peoples of the Mesopotamian plains and highlands, in an area extending to modern-day south-eastern Turkey, north-eastern Syria, northern Iraq, north-western Iran and beyond to south-western Armenia.

when he began to receive signals from Cecil Edmunds, his assistant who by now was APO at Ranya. Edmunds was increasingly concerned about the growing impact of Turkish and hostile tribal agitation in Rowanduz District to the north, which he believed was aimed at an uprising in Kurdistan. This then developed into a full-blown invasion which overwhelmed the limited forces available to resist. After much prevarication, and ably supported by Horace, it was finally decided to send a small force of Levies—i.e. locally recruited troops[6]—and a few Sikhs to retake Ranya late in August 1922. This failed completely.

Having ejected Edmunds and his British colleagues from Ranya at the end of August, the Turks and Kurdish rebels occupied a small town called Koi from which they intended to threaten Sulaimania itself. The ranks of rebel tribesmen were growing, notably among the Pizdhars.[7] It was at this point that the RAF mounted an offensive against the enemy parties at Ranya and Marga that then spread to Pizdhar villages and the Shawur valleys to the north that marked the Turkish main lines of communication with Rowanduz.[8] No. 6 Squadron's detachment to Kirkuk was one of the components of this thrust.

Horace was deeply involved. This was happening on his doorstep or, more to the point, on *ours*. He would call on the RAF to strike at tribal threats from time to time and was certainly one of those who believed that bombing was the only way to impose civilisation on the tribes in the region. I wasn't sure what I thought about this. He called it 'aerial policing'.

It all came to a head after about six months, when joint

---

[6] During the British Mandate in Iraq in the 1920s, Levies were used to support British administrative and military efforts. They included Assyrian Christians, Kurds, Arabs, and other local groups.

[7] Also spelled Pizhdars.

[8] Initiated by Air Vice Marshall Sir John Salmond, who had just taken over responsibility for military control in Iraq.

Kurd and Turk fighters threw us out of Ranya. They easily overcame a rather weak British attempt to regain the town and, in Horace's words, 'something had to be done ... .'

Before I say anything else, you must forgive me for not really understanding the politics that drove the establishment of Iraq. I did know that the Turks refused to accept that Mosul Province, which included Sulaimania Liwa, was no longer part of the Ottoman Empire; added to this, that the Kurds yearned for an independent Kurdistan in lands that straddled Turkey and northern Iraq, which included much of Mosul. The Turks could not resist the temptation to exploit this. They stirred up rebellious Kurdish tribes not far to the north of us, as a result of which we now we faced a full-blown invasion led by a man called Shaikh Mahmud who set himself up as champion of the Kurds and set his sights on Sulaimania.

As we were right in the path of the Kurds and their thirst for independence, the RAF flew the British residents of Sulaimania to Kirkuk by air on 3 September 1922 in huge aeroplanes called Vernons—noisy things.[9] Horace helped to organise it. And what drama! There was a splash about it in the *Illustrated London News* that got Daddy all excited. We both went straight on to Baghdad. Just as well, as I was seven months pregnant.

I gave birth to David Armstrong Goldsmith at a hospital in Baghdad on 28 October 1922. He was adorable—all six pounds of him. Horace was thrilled.

The birth spawned a flurry of letters from a delighted family at home. In a funny sort of way, I think that David's arrival made our marriage a little more respectable. Was this the beginning of some sort of rehabilitation? Judging by the welcome we received the next summer, I think it was.

---

[9] This was the first time that the RAF carried out an air evacuation.

David Armstrong Goldsmith, aged fourteen days, 11 November 1922.

Angela was full of herself for other reasons. I sensed her triumph when she sent me a cutting from the local paper that had trumpeted Mama's usual Christmas dance—this time at the Princes Hotel. As daughter of one of the three hostesses, Angela had taken centre stage in a classy outfit—'elegantly gowned in soft-jade-green draperies of georgette, with a bandeau encircling her dark hair'. My, my—and still not twenty-one!

While all this was going on, Baghdad was abuzz with talk of the crisis in the East. We heard that the RAF was throwing everything it had into bombing the Turks and rebel Kurds around Ranya and that, by the New Year, some of the tribal leaders who had sided with Shaikh Mahmud had shifted away from him. The word in Baghdad was that the shaikh was on the run, that the RAF was hunting him down and that peace was restored. Or so it seemed.

Harry was one of those in the thick of the bombing campaign. He flew rickety planes called Bristol Fighters and his squadron was shifted from Baghdad to Kirkuk to be closer to its targets.

Kirkuk was a dusty dump, a far cry from the big oil town that it would later turn out to be. It sounded as though the troops and expats there had a thin time as far as entertainment went and they began to trickle into Baghdad in search of fun when there were lulls in flying.

And that is how I met Harry again. We came across each other during one of his trips and I invited him for tea at the Alwiyah Club (*see page 44–45*), a new spot on the banks of the Tigris where the Brits tended to congregate. He didn't need much persuasion and even young David's bawling didn't put him off. I do have to admit that, lacking many kindred spirits in Iraq, I felt very refreshed (even if not tempted) by this young, energetic and handsome man. And he *did* turn out to be a lovely dancer.

After that I met Harry several times again at various social functions. He still spent most of his time chasing and bombing Kurds in the hills—pretty dangerous stuff—but in Baghdad he could let off steam. I remember dancing with him when he came into Baghdad with an Air Force crowd and confiding with him that one of his friends had upset me by trying to hold my hand. I knew he liked me, but he was most respectful. I imagined he had plenty of opportunities to cross boundaries elsewhere.

The Alwiyah club, Baghdad: winter 1922–23

Harry was funny and full of tales of his flying exploits. The thing that he talked about most was chasing gazelles on the ground or huge birds in the air while his observer shot at them. Years later he showed me a splendid photograph showing him and his observer posing with one of the greater bustards they had shot down and picked up—the wings were more than four feet across. He was particularly proud of his catch of gazelles, which he said can run at 45 mph and more. As I got to know him better I realised that he was very much a hunter at heart.

He had some hilarious tales of the pranks they would play on each other, to ease the boredom at Kirkuk—some of them wildly improbable. I remember one about an officer lobbing lit Chinese crackers into his friends' tents at night and scaring them witless; I wasn't sure how much of it to believe.

Around March they began a big push to quieten the Kurds and turf the Turks out of the area around Ranya and Rowanduz. It lasted a few months and Harry and his comrades were flying day-in and day-out, supporting the troops on the ground. In Baghdad we were relieved to hear good news: the operation was going successfully.

As for our relationship, it was all perfectly respectable and we did exchange a few letters while he was stuck out at Kirkuk.

The following May we sailed for England, landing at London in early June. Daddy, now over the angst that followed my departure, was hugely relieved to have me out of harm's way (as he saw it) and peace was restored among the Copemans.

The summer flew by: I remember reunions in Sussex, family hols in Scotland and frivolity in London. Then Horace sailed to India, and made for a town called Tonk, in Rajputana, where he was to be the revenue officer. I followed on New Years' Day 1924 with David and his nurse and we did our best to make the most of the short time we spent there.

An old walled town, Tonk was the main city of a princely state that had existed for ages.[10] It boasted some fine old mosques and some elegant houses that they called *havelis*—one of which we lived in. We were about fifty miles south of the bigger city of Jaipur. There was not much between the two places apart from desert and the Bana river that curled lazily around the northern fringe of our town.

While Horace had had to endure the last months of the rains, it was winter when I arrived and we were to leave just before the rains began. By then, of course, the heat had really brewed up and my attempts to arrange a veil around my *topi* did little to cool me down or slow the steady trickle of dust down my back and the irresistible urge to sneeze.

I also had to get used to completely different food—the Indians' fierce curries that were tasty but provoked yet more sneezing. Thankfully I escaped the 'Delhi belly' that everyone had warned me about. I must have had a cast-iron gut.

---

[10] The Princely State of Tonk consisted of several areas of modern-day Rajasthan and Central India. Tonk was its capital in the British times.

It was all very different from Baghdad. Talking of which, I think that Harry was still there, probably with plenty to do and other things on his mind. So I wrote to him once or twice—just to distract him a little.

Chapter 5
Harry in Kurdistan

> Aircrews could be happy or heedless killers
> who talked about machine-gunning a village
> as if they recounted shooting a buck or a bird
> on a hunting trip. They were also mostly
> admirable, honourable and idealistic young men,
> among the best of their generation, who believed
> they were serving their country, the grace of God
> and even those they bombed. The use of
> weapons ranging from bombs to incendiary
> devices to chastise primitive people in the
> name of civilisation, however, is not a comfortable
> subject. Modern readers are likely to cringe at
> the prejudice and callousness that imbued
> the Empire's rulers.
>
> BARRY RENFREW, *WINGS OF EMPIRE*, P.15

[Author's Note: Up to this point Margaret's tales had been a beacon of clarity: memory sharp, sequence of events correct, delights and angsts all spelled out coherently. But now some aspects of her recollection failed her. She had wanted to talk about Harry's early days in Kurdistan but got hopelessly muddled: events in the wrong order, details akimbo, vagueness all round. This would not do.

I have tried to remedy this. Armed with her letters, a few research tools and the gift of some spare time to put it all together, I think that the following—in my words—presents a more accurate picture of what happened next in his life.]

Harry Reid (ringed), with his flight and an F2B, RAF Hinaidi, 1922.

Having danced between the Unemployed and Active lists of the RAF in the wake of the redundancies of 1919, Harry was recalled for a refresher flying course in May 1921. The following January he was on his way to Iraq where he joined No. 6 Squadron in April 1922 and began the best part of three years as a Bristol Fighter pilot, based initially at Hinaidi cantonment on the southeast outskirts of Baghdad. He was twenty-two.

The Bristol F2B Fighter was a highly successful two-seat biplane that came into Royal Flying Corps's operational service in 1917. Affectionately known as 'Brisfits' or 'Biffs', the BF aircraft was used extensively in light bombing, reconnaissance and general army cooperation roles.[1] In Kurdistan and elsewhere in the Middle East it was considered a key contributor to the RAF's success in its aerial policing.[2] Surprisingly for a two-seater, the plane was very manoeuvrable. It was armed with a forward-firing Vickers machine gun operated by the pilot and one or two Lewis guns mounted on a gun support frame in the observer's cockpit. Racks fitted below the lower wing carried a maximum bomb load of 240 lbs. More often than not, Harry's bombload in Kurdistan would consist of eight 20 lb 'Cooper' bombs or, occasionally, much larger numbers of small incendiary devices.

Fatal crashes in two of the squadron's BFs soon after Harry's arrival at Hinaidi provided stark reminders of the hazards of flying these relatively crude aircraft.

While the RAF station at Hinaidi was new and fairly well appointed, the old hands who were used to the informality of desert operations further afield found the return to parade-

---

[1] Army cooperation relates to RAF squadrons tasked specifically with working closely with and in support of the British Army.

[2] Others (such as Priya Satia, 2006) would later question the use of the word 'success' in this context.

ground ritual that went with their new surroundings somewhat tiresome. They also had to tolerate an influx of new (and in their view inexperienced) pilots, of whom Harry was one. Alan Shipwright—a 'card' if there ever was one—was another; Harry would later shortlist him when choosing a best man, only to conclude that his ability to spring surprises posed too great a risk and that a safer pair of hands might prove wiser.

Harry's first six months allowed him to 'learn' his aircraft and the region: weaponry, navigation, sketching uncharted areas, coping with forced landings and other challenges, all leading to his first bombing raid on 5 October 1922. The next day he left the relative comfort of Hinaidi and transferred to the squadron's detachment at Kirkuk, to support the British operations against rebellious Kurds in the Sulaimania region.

Harry won no prizes for cottoning on that his new surroundings were a touch primitive after the relative luxury of Hinaidi. A reasonable-sized town with a population of around 25,000 at the time, Kirkuk lies on a plain that stretches between a relatively low ridge to the west, called the Hamrin, and the great mountains of Kurdistan that ring it to the north and east. As the crow flies it lies about 150 miles from Baghdad but flight distances between the two exceeded 200 miles, as the Rolls Royce engines that powered the BF would fail from time to time, forcing pilots to keep within gliding distance of settlements. Sulaimania is some sixty miles east of Kirkuk. Apart from the odd holes in the ground from which inhabitants could extract crude oil, there was no hint of the booming oil town that would evolve some ten years later.

At a pinch you might call the station 'semi-permanent;' it consisted of a mudbrick *serai* [caravanserai] close to the airfield, within which the aircraft were parked at night, and a series of tents that provided mess accommodation.

Temperatures ranged from fierce heat in the summer to shivering cold in the winter. Added to this, inactivity and sexual frustration were rife among the all-male RAF personnel, which provided ammunition for pranksters: anything to liven up the proceedings. But at least the relative informality on the station was a welcome change from the ceremony and drills that had prevailed at Hinaidi. And apart from paying one's bar bills, there was little scope for spending money.

One notable prankster was David d'Arcy Greig, a flight commander who was obsessed with pyrotechnics and went to some extremes to alleviate the monotony of Kirkuk. At some point he discovered that there were fish in the network of *qanats* through which water flowed from the hills to the north of the airfield, and he had a go at killing them with a 20 lb 'Cooper' bomb, for the hell of it. When the explosion achieved nothing bar destroying a piece of antiquity and terrifying a nearby Arab, he decided to focus instead on his fellow officers. All members of the detachment slept on camp beds in small tents pitched in the serai, and relied on oil lamps that cast shadows on the tent walls, making it easy to see their movements from outside. Greig's idea was to lob a lit Chinese cracker into an occupant's bath as he performed his evening ablutions, and enjoy the ensuing panic. While the miscreant was soon uncovered; information on the revenge that his fellow officers exacted on him is hidden … .

During the cooler months the shooting season came as a welcome distraction for Harry and his comrades. They could pick up snipe and duck from the nearby waterways and black partridges and woodcock from more organised shoots further afield.

From Kirkuk Harry flew a wide range of anti-tribal bombing and other missions as part of an air policing role that focused initially on Marga and Pizdhar, two subdivisions in Ranya District either side of the Little Zab river. He was one of several pilots who flew the political officer Cecil Edmonds, using his intimate knowledge of the peoples and terrain below

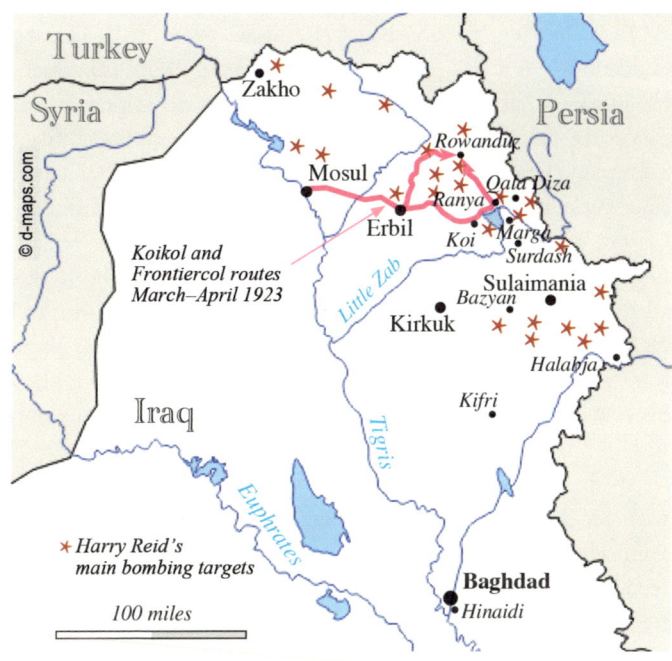

No. 6 Squadron's area of operations in Kurdistan, 1922–24.

to guide the British retaliation effort against the Turks and the Pizdhars in and around their base at Qala Diza. As Harry's observer on the first bombing raid on Marga town on 27 October, Edmunds recalled:

> We started the intensive bombing of Marga today. I went up to point out the targets. My pilot, McLaren-Reid, did some beautiful shooting; one 'cooper' in particular burst in the doorway of the serai and ought to have done some damage. The sensation of bombing is exhilarating as you cruise over your target and after each discharge heel over to look down on your handiwork before working round to repeat the attack.
>
> CECIL EDMUNDS, *KURDS, TURKS, AND ARABS*, P.299

In *Wings of Empire* Barry Renfrew notes that Horace Goldsmith was a strong advocate of bombing errant tribesmen. He insisted that 'bombing was the only way to impose civilisation on the tribes in the region he had administered' from Sulaimani, from where he and Margaret had been evacuated four weeks before Harry and his colleagues moved to Kirkuk.

The raids continued into the New Year. As well as retaliating from the ground with rifles and machine guns, the Kurds adapted captured mountain guns for anti-aircraft work, and Harry, for one, reported shell bursts near him. Inevitably there were casualties: a pilot from No. 1 Squadron was killed when his Sopwith Snipe was shot down over Ranya by machine gun fire.

In time the bombing led some tribal leaders who had sided with Shaikh Mahmud to withdraw their support and realign themselves with the British and so weaken the shaikh's resources. By now he had set himself up as the figurehead of free Kurdistan and, to the irritation of many of his fellow Kurds, finally exposed his alignment with the Turks. The British hunted him relentlessly, but without success.

Barely had the Ranya threat been tackled when there came a specific and greater joint Kurdish–Turk menace from Turkish irregular troops in the Rowanduz area and warlike Pizdhar tribesmen in the area near Ranya close to the border with Persia. In his determination to stamp British authority in the region, AVM Salmond[3] determined to hold down the Pizdhar around Ranya, prevent them from assisting in the Rowanduz area and drive a wedge between Shaikh Mahmud and the Turks. His tactic was to send two columns of troops tasked with taking the town of Rowanduz in a pincer move; the first, called 'Koicol', marched from Mosul on 18 March, followed eight

---

[3] Air Vice Marshall Sir John Salmond was the first RAF officer to be given command of all British Forces, both land and air, in a particular area—in this case Iraq.

days later by the second, called 'Frontiercol'. Koicol would deal with the Pizdhar while Frontiercol would take Rowanduz from the west.

After advancing through very hostile and difficult terrain, the two columns linked and occupied Rowanduz on 22 April and in due course Shaikh Mahmud's support crumbled. He fled into Persia and the British reoccupied Sulaimania on 17 May 1923. AVM Salmond recorded that it was largely 'due to those air attacks directed against Shaikh Mahmud and his forces that he was unable either to perfect his organisation or to raise the tribes for resistance to the columns'.

No. 6 Squadron's role in these operations was first to harass Shaikh Mahmud in Surdash district and then to co-operate with Koicol once it reached Koi (which it did on 4 April 1923). Chasing the shaikh and bombing the places where he was thought to be continued all the time.

Harry recorded nothing in his logbooks to suggest any derring-do. His remarks are brief and factual, preferring instead to focus more on non-military matters ('shot a greater bustard. Landed and picked it up'), bringing in emergency supplies of beer, or being carpeted by his CO for low flying.

But there are hints: his entry for 25 February 1923—'led formation of Vernons to Sal.[4] On way landed to pick up Roberts. Vernon got bogged'—thinly disguises his role in a second attempt to airlift a party of 14th Sikhs from Kifri to reinforce Kirkuk. This involved twelve BFs and four twin-engined Vickers Vernons and at one point it was reported that seven of the machines were down in the Bazyan valley; one BF had forced-landed with engine trouble and Harry had landed alongside to help. Despite his warning signals one of the heavy Vernons landed and was bogged down; then more BFs. Eventually all got off except the Vernon, which eventually required a complicated salvage effort.

---

[4] Sal is short for Sulaimania.

Harry's work was varied: bombing and strafing villages, shooting cattle, hunting for Shaikh Mahmud and his followers, dropping leaflets and supporting the ground troops throughout their areas of operation. In the absence of wireless, he became something of an expert at picking up messages: during the Koicol operations he 'caught' the orders to commence air-support hanging in a bag suspended between two treetops using a grapnel[5] let down over the side of his aircraft —the first time he had tried this. Just imagine such a Heath Robinson arrangement. ... His logbook entry for that day simply reads, 'Koicol—picked up mail'.

And why drop leaflets? When reports of the indiscriminate bombing of Turkish villagers began to reach London, they provoked criticism. One response was to drop warning leaflets *in advance* of the raids (regarded by some as very counter-productive).

Flying was difficult in Kurdistan's mountains, which rise to 8,000 ft. In addition to the inherent dangers of bad weather, mechanical failure, pilot error and enemy fire, planes had to follow valleys and dodge between the mountain peaks as part of their ground support work. Harry certainly had his fair share of forced landings; a story that surfaced many years later held that the local shaikh offered him one of his daughters as a bride after one such event.

By the time that the Kirkuk Detachment returned to Hinaidi in August 1923 Harry had flown 401 hours and carried out eighty-four bombing raids from Kirkuk on over thirty targets. He and his colleagues had done well: ten months later the *London Gazette* announced the award of the Distinguished Flying Cross (D.F.C.) for 'distinguished service rendered during the operations in Kurdistan between 15 February and 19 June

---

[5] A small anchor or grappling hook with multiple prongs, typically used for climbing, rescue missions or retrieving objects.

1923' to six RAF officers, and Harry was one of them. His citation reads:

> For gallantry and devotion to duty. This officer has flown over 304 hours during operations. He has always shown great daring in actions and a complete disregard for his own safety. He has on many occasions carried out low flying in the face of rifle and machine gun fire from the ground.

Alongside the officers were six NCO observers, one of whom (Charles Dix) flew regularly with Harry, who received the Distinguished Flying Medal.

From all this we must conclude that Harry was something of a daredevil, over and above the routine hazards of flying. But perhaps this is less surprising when one remembers that he had grown up in the wild as a young cowboy in Argentina.

It is also perhaps not surprising that Harry was just as interested in his hunting achievements as his bombing when he summarised his efforts in his log book, in which one entry reads: 'Carried out 84 bomb raids from Kirkuk, landed and brought back 12 gazelle shot by observer. Ditto 4 greater bustard.'

Back at Hinaidi it was time for the squadron to recuperate after ten months under canvas—and the fleshpots of Baghdad were not far away. Close at hand too, was the Alwiyah club, a relatively new establishment on the banks of the Tigris where Margaret Goldsmith would some time later entertain Harry to tea. It is not difficult to imagine that she found relatively few kindred spirits in Iraq and that most of those she met were older than she was: how easy for her to be refreshed—even if not tempted—by such a young, energetic and handsome man (and vice versa).

In May 1924 No. 6 Squadron moved to Mosul, an ancient city where the aerodrome was sited at the edge of an old fort and accommodation—for the officers at least—was far better than at Kirkuk.

Harry had barely settled down to these relative comforts when he received a letter from Margaret written from Tonk: it certainly got him thinking.

He had met Margaret in Sulaimania a couple of years earlier and while there were no family or close-friend connections, they subsequently caught up with each other at social functions in Baghdad. They could both be described as 'beautiful' people of the times, he just one year older.

They would certainly have remembered each other. So what prompted her to write again? Was she 'fishing' or just honing her flirtation skills at long range? Whatever the answer, I suspect that she was tiring of army life and sought some kind of distraction from the quiet of Tonk.

Harry's first letter to her from Mosul is full of allusion to action. He is very much alive, while not entirely sure what is going on as far as she is concerned. He asks after her and her son—but not about her husband. He is curious and would like to meet. At this moment he has no particular hopes to keep at bay.

At that point he could have had no inkling of the tragedy that was about to strike Margaret, and the impact that this would have on them both in the longer term.

But that's enough from me for now. It's time to return to Margaret's words and events that she recalled only too keenly.

Chapter 6
Young widow

In future I am going to call you Margaret unless, of course, you strongly object but you won't will you? I've known you for ever so long; and incidentally you make an awful mouthful of my name. Thank you ever so much for your very nice long letter—not the one you sent from India: that has not arrived yet although I expect it will later on. ...

At present we are at a place called Zakho, keeping an eye on the Turks of whom you have no doubt heard. At the beginning of the operations we had great fun with them and they certainly got the worst of it—now everything is peaceful again and we are expecting to return to Mosul any time.

None of us will be sorry because it will soon be most uncomfortable and cold in these tents. Two days ago the first of the rains started and we were frozen; today however is wonderful.

HARRY TO ME, 30 OCTOBER 1924

We stayed in Tonk until May when we were due for more leave. We all set off for Bombay and were soon at sea again, this time on a mail steamer called *Caledonia*. But Horace's health crumbled once on board. He had been unwell for a while and following an unusually successful hand or two of bridge he collapsed one evening at dinner. I got him into bed, propped him up and called the ship's doctor who promptly scolded me for not having done so sooner. What I didn't realise was how sick he was. The doc was very pessimistic and did his best to make him comfortable with morphine (I think)—but in vain. Horace was nauseous, weak with a very high temperature and the most dreadful headache. What was worse, the doc wouldn't let me near him—said that whatever he had might be contagious. I couldn't even hold his hand.

He died on 31 May. They thought that he had meningitis and that sepsis had set in. It was horribly quick.

We were less than half-way home and I went to pieces. Horace was only thirty-seven. They offloaded us at Suez, where they buried him with obscene haste; they did their best, but nothing felt 'normal' about the process. The ship's chaplain followed rituals handed down through generations of seafarers and while he involved me as much as he could there was almost nothing for me to decide. The sight of his coffin sinking into the ground haunted me for ages. What to do? I felt paralysed.

We returned to the ship, somehow got as far as the other end of the Mediterranean and disembarked at Marseilles. You know, I think the other passengers were glad to have us out of the way. Daddy was there to meet us and managed to get us back to Hove, refuge and Mama.

I remember nothing. All a ghastly blur. Mercifully, sister Angela and various friends were close by. Rose, David's nanny, was a brick—poor little mite, he was not even two and must have been completely foxed by it all.

Daddy, bless him, had kept my allowance going, so what with that and Horace's pension I was able to stay afloat. All the same, the lights went out as far as I was concerned and I dreaded being alone at night. Hated widow's weeds. Hated being thought of as a 'widow' for that matter.

After a life-saving spell of parental care, little David and I returned to our empty house at 21, Wilbury Crescent [Hove]. And there on the door mat, I found a letter from Harry—

written about a week before Horace died and imagining that we were already home. I didn't really register it at first and it took me a couple of months to reply.

Slowly I began to recover. Angela was a great help but wouldn't stop reminding me that feeling sorry for myself was *verboten* (which of course meant that I bottled the whole thing up even more and alcohol became even more of a friend). Alright for her—barely twenty-one and so full of zip. But, in spite of my uselessness at cards, she even got me back at the bridge table *and* she did get me out of the house, dragging me in search of clothes or to some tennis party or other. I even managed to brave a dance or two.

Her moment of triumph came when she persuaded me to join her for a holiday in Dieppe; in spite of my initial misgivings it posed an alternative to gin and turned out to be good fun).

David meanwhile was growing. Now a toddler, he was happy in the garden and (so everyone said) very bright. While he didn't understand what was going on he did realise now that his daddy wasn't coming home.

At some point I remembered Harry's letter. It was no more than a kindly enquiry about how we were and gentle chit-chat about mutual friends and what was happening in Sulaimania (they were bombing the place) and I thought that the least I could do was to tell him about Horace. So I did. As I did want him to write again, I said that I was beginning to get back to some sort of normal and face the world. And maybe deep down there was more to it than that …

Well, Harry replied by the nearest that you could get to 'return', when you consider sea mail. His letter read:

Mosul, 12.8.24

My dear Mrs Goldsmith

I can't tell you how sorry I was to hear of your husband's death and I want to express my deepest sympathy. It must have been terrible for you. It was a shock for me too because I knew him well at Slemani and liked him very much indeed.

I am glad that you are now going about a little and looking on the brighter side of things.

I have only just returned from a fortnight's leave up to the Persian Border which I enjoyed immensely—no it had nothing to do with the Munroes, accounts of whom you have heard from Sir Berkeley Vincent[6]—so he told you all about how sad and depressed I was, did he? I guarantee however, that he did not tell you his own feelings in the matter, perhaps he will some day when he feels confidential, very confidential.

Returning to the subject of my leave—we flew from here to Rowanduz and then went with two companies of Assyrian Levies all over the most wonderful country chiefly where no Britisher had been before.

On average we did seven hours riding each day except for two days when we had to walk the whole time, the road being much too steep to ride.

On the last day another fellow and I climbed up to 9,000 ft. (it nearly killed me trying to keep up with our six Assyrian Levies who acted as a guard). We then slept on a grass bed in our shorts and two blankets and nearly got frozen to death for there still was an appreciable amount of snow.

Nevertheless, it was well worth it—the next morning we managed to shoot three ibex which was what we originally set out to do.

Altogether I took ninety-five photographs, the negatives of which I saw yesterday, most of them excellent.

I am so glad to learn that David is flourishing, he must be quite big now and quite different to the small bundle

---

[6] Commander of British Forces in Iraq, 1922–24

One of the first two 'snapshots' with Harry, on the left, at Kirkuk.

that I used to know as David, I always remember him screaming the place down when I came to tea with you one day at the Alwiyah Club.

There is now a rumour that seven of us who have done three years out here are to be sent to Egypt or India—I hope I am not one of them, but we shall know in about a week's time. I want to be sent home for a year and then go abroad again. One of the chief objections to England is the damnable weather, don't you think so?

Au revoir please write again soon.

Yours very sincerely H McLaren Reid

PS I enclose two snapshots taken some time ago at Slemani.

I remember thinking 'what a curious mixture'. Sympathy—yes, but it didn't take him long to launch into tales of *his* adventures.

I did like the photographs—he looked particularly dishy in one. Come to think of it, what better way to arouse my curiosity? So I sent him a long letter telling him about my holiday in Dieppe and my tentative steps towards 'men', just to tease him a bit.

That really got him going. He replied like lightning, telling me how he was suffering in some god-forsaken place called Zakho up near the Turkish border. Apparently the Turks had planned to cross the border and seize the town and Harry's squadron had been sent to sort them out.

But as Daddy reminded me (his eagle eye scanning the papers as keenly as ever) the RAF's policy of killing innocent Kurdish villagers in the hills and deliberately targeting their livestock was not his idea of cricket.

And Harry was unquestionably part of this. Unscathed by frequent enemy machine gun fire he drily noted that he had 'killed sheik's son and three of his wives'. I never quite worked out what he really thought about this. After all, 'orders were

No. 6 SQUADRON,
ROYAL AIR FORCE,
MOSUL,
IRAQ.

30.10.24.

My dear Mrs Edward Margaret

In future I am going to call you Margaret unless, of course, you strongly object but you won't will you? I've known you for ever so long; and incidently you make an awful mouthful of my name.

Thank you ever so much for your very nice long letter — not the one you sent to India, that has not arrived yet although I expect it will later on.

I have at last got a photograph of your husband's house in

	Zakho detachment.				
18.9.24	Self	4727	Sgt Dix	1.0	Mosul to Zakho
19.9.24	"	"	Brown	2.10	Recon police posts, found Rekan burning and Turkish encampment with tents and horse lines.
19.9.24	"	"	"	2.10	Recon Challek & Bahita
19.9.24	"	"	"	50	Bombed Shersini. Troops & pack animals bolted under [illeg]
20.9.24	"	"	"	2.45	Located large body of troops & horses at Drell. i-masak[?] with machine guns. Bombed & machine gunned them. Concent[rated] 7 [illeg] 29,000 [illeg] of Turkish [illeg] 40 horses killed 5 Turks & 50 Turks wounded.
21.9.24	"	"	Sgt Hamlin	50	Z.M. to bring M du & Remains to Zakho with P.Dest[?]
22.9.24	"	"	A/C Penrice	3	Centre section loose & engine dud
22.9.24	"	"	Hurd	15	Engine test

Top: Harry's letter to me from Zakho. Above: from Harry's log book.

orders' and he was paid to 'do' rather than 'think'. But did that even *begin* to sound like an excuse?

What was worse, or at least confusing, was his later revelation that he had also killed horses (the Turkish troops he and his flight were hunting were cavalrymen). Just how did he square his lifelong affection for animals with shooting horses? Was there some sort of partition in his brain that separated his natural affections from the requirement to obey orders?

Chapter 7
Life begins to return

> I envy you going to all these dances, will you be
> available about the middle of January when I get
> home? I have to be in Egypt in five weeks' time to
> catch the troopship from Port Said.
> HARRY TO ME, 9 NOVEMBER 1925

Christmas and the seasonal rituals approached. By now I had been home for about six months and I did my best to 'fit in'. Somehow I managed to endure all the people at Daddy and Mama's silver wedding celebration at the end of the year, a grand bash they held at the Metropole Hotel in Brighton. Of course (form and all that) I was obliged to wear black, leaving Angela to steal the limelight (in a rather glorious pink if I'm not mistaken). Grim ...

But there was a rather hilarious side-effect. We were both invited to be mannequins at a London department store—showing off new fashions and all that. Very flattering of course and one or two of our friends had already dipped their toes in this pond. But it was not to be: Mama would have had the vapours—completely non-U!

As far as Harry was concerned, I can't really remember what happened next. I think I must have cooled off a bit. Well, who wants to get too side-tracked by someone miles away who might or might not appear for ages, however gorgeous?

Then around six months later I weakened and wrote at length. This prompted a surprised but happy reply mixing the drear of Cairo with various adventures, and envy about all the dances I had attended (v. flattering), complaining because I still hadn't sent him a photograph (v.v. flattering) and fearing that I would have remarried before he got back to England.

> You seem to be thoroughly enjoying yourself—I wish I could be stationed somewhere near you and take you to all these dances, but I suppose that by the time I get back you will have married again and be too engrossed with your husband to have time to go anywhere.
>
> HARRY TO ME, 2 JUNE 1925

Then all went quiet; weeks and then a month or two passed and no word. Harry had during this time returned to aerial policing, not that I knew this then—this time in the Yemen, bombing what we used to call 'unruly' tribes north of Aden.

It only emerged later that he had become entangled with a vamp called 'Peter' in Aden, so he had other things on his mind than me. Years later Harry admitted that he had met an old Aden hand who reminded him that he had force-landed on

Harry inspecting the wreckage of a crashed aircraft: Aden, 1925.

the coast and sent a message to his 'little lovely' in Aden by writing on the sand for the pilot of another machine to read—apparently the talk of the town for ages).[7]

And as for me—well I should come clean. I was equally distracted. Angela had introduced me to an interesting chap called Bonzo; not quite as good-looking or dashing as Harry but very well-heeled. What made him even more interesting was that he was just around the corner, and therefore well worth my attention. I even gave him a copy of my photograph: it hit him like a ton of bricks. (Victim Number Two.)

But why let Harry off my nice long lead? We exchanged a few more letters and I read more of his adventures, one minute bombing more local tribesmen ('unruly', of course) and the next having exotic holidays in the Red Sea, promising all the while that he would soon be back in England. What with being shot at and frequent forced landings, it all sounded hellish dangerous. I think he came close to a second DFC for what his superior officers described as his 'skill and keenness' during these operations. Talking of the DFC, he kept very quiet about it in his letters. And he was always on the move:

> In a fortnight's time I am off to Somaliland for three months where there is good lion and leopard shooting so here's hoping that they call on my bungalow and then come home with me in the form of rugs. I think you ought to let your house and help me to shoot them!
>
> HARRY TO ME, 30 SEPTEMBER 1925

So I sent him a copy of the photograph too. (I knew he would become Victim Number Three). Well that certainly did the trick: he was ecstatic. On the other hand, he was far less happy about his arrival in Somaliland when:

---

[7] The event took place on 13 October 1925 on Harry's way back from a bombing raid.

Half-way there (from Berbera port) it started to rain and the driver said he would not be able to get through, however we told him to go on—soon afterwards we came to a river with the water pelting down, the water stopped the engine half-way across and also took the Ford a few yards downstream. We eventually got it out with the help of some forty natives!

A few miles further the car gave up the ghost but luckily a Ford passed us, so I travelled in that until we met an enormous rock which had fallen on to the pass, the only thing to do then was to walk which I did for two and a half hours—in the pitch-dark arriving at eleven o'clock soaked to the skin and cold as charity.

HARRY TO ME, 9 NOVEMBER 1925

This gloom didn't dampen his delight in arriving at an abundance of vegetation and 'birds of all colours and shapes', after the emptiness of Aden. And it certainly didn't stop him from reminding me how he envied my social life.

Talking of which, I now had Bonzo in focus. And yes, it was time for some fun ...

Perhaps I should introduce you to Bonzo? His real name was George Drew Fanshawe and at the time we met he was a lieutenant in the Royal Horse Artillery. He was a year younger than me and was from a rather unusual family. His father, Edward Cardwell Fanshawe, was the son of Admiral Sir Edward Gennys Fanshawe G.C.B. GCB? Crikey! That's a Knight Grand Cross of the Order of the Bath, the highest rank of the Most Honourable Order of the Bath. (Why the bath? Oh, they're terribly pure, those knights. Or they were in medieval times, when they swore allegiance to the king. They're probably smellier these days, especially on active duty on the high seas.)

The Fanshawes oozed military blood from every pore—admirals and generals everywhere. Edward, an army engineer, had only got as far as lieutenant colonel while Bonzo's uncle

'We met at a dance in Brighton in '25. Somehow he was different.'

Arthur became an Admiral of the Fleet. After his first wife divorced him in the 1880s (for habitual adultery) Edward married Alice Drew in 1900 and Bonzo was their first child. Bonzo's father died in 1917, leaving the improbably large sum of almost £48,000[8] to Alice. Bonzo and his younger sister Kathleen glided into financial clover.

Educated at Tonbridge (not quite Eton but still fairly pukka), he followed in the family footsteps and headed straight for the army. Not sure why he didn't become a cavalryman (pretty good on a horse) but in truth he just wasn't flash. He was tall, good-looking and generous to a fault—cut quite a dash. Funny, too. Not quite so fancy on the dance floor but still passable. Mixed an explosive cocktail. (Like it or not my cosy relationship with alcohol was here to stay.)

We met at a dance in Brighton in '25. Somehow he was different; not full of swagger like most of the other men who 'had a go'. You know, I had him hooked without even trying.

---

[8] Around £3.4 million at 2021 prices.

He was—how to say—vulnerable, a mixture of proper and polite. He was surprisingly gentle for a soldier. Our one big disagreement was over my smoking which he didn't like—and he thought that long cigarette holders were vulgar.

He was stationed at Aldershot and thought nothing of driving down to Hove for the weekend. Sometimes we met in London where he had a clutch of fairly wild friends; all very respectable though—I would stay with Grandmama, who in her own way encouraged me to keep up my escape from widow's weeds. Hyde Park was but a stone's throw away and I could wander there in glorious anonymity. Once let loose I found London out of this world—made Hove seem quite provincial; theatre, dance, glamour, delicious men, wild hair styles—and clothes (quite my weak spot).

And then Harry landed on my doorstep …

Chapter 8
Rivals: Harry vs Bonzo

> How is Bonzo? ... of course, he is the lucky devil just now, sort of a ding-dong battle this, though it will be my turn again next weekend—sounds bad doesn't it!
> HARRY TO ME, 15 FEBRUARY 1926

Harry's troopship from Port Said landed him at Southampton in the middle of January 1926. He was just twenty-seven, had been away for four years and was quite unprepared for the 'Roaring Twenties' that ate him up whole. While he couldn't wait to see me, I viewed this moment with a mixture of excitement and dread; was it to be quite delicious or a dreadful anti-climax?

Well, it had to be faced and sensing my excitement, Mama and Daddy invited Harry to stay with them at Brunswick Square (what better way to vet him?). So one cold wet morning, in he walked waving flowers for Mama (the charmer —must have been born to it). He was as tall as I remembered and still decidedly good-looking, sun tan and all. Irresistible. But for me it was really difficult. I so wanted to touch him but the weight of still having to play the merry widow with all those other eyes looking at me really mucked that up. What had happened to yesterday's rebel? Why was I suddenly worried about appearances?

Harry was on his best behaviour. Having banked about three years of salary he was also relatively flush, so no one realised that he would be short of the stuff for years to come.

He enthralled Mama, Daddy and everyone else with his

tales of the mystic east (better at stories than me) and took a real liking to little David. Angela gave him good marks. At some point later I introduced him to Grandmama and they got on like a house on fire.

The Brighton lanes worked their magic—that maze of little streets that tie the railway station to the sea; very picturesque. I suppose you might call it 'Old Brighton'—surrounded by the rather nasty new town that mushroomed around it. From a place where the fishermen lived, it had shifted to a hotchpotch of curiosity shops and second-hand book stalls—we were almost back in Baghdad *souks*.

Somehow what might have been a couple of very sticky days stretched into two weeks of fun, excitement, discovery and delight. I even introduced Harry to Bonzo but he wasn't fazed (to begin with, at least).

We explored Sussex, we walked and talked, danced once or twice. I bought him a tie.

At some point Harry's 'little' brother Toby appeared.[9] Together they took the train back to London at the end of the month and took up rooms in a grand old building in Bayswater, just off Hyde Park shared by a lively group of young men.

I did not know what to think. The intensity of our relationship burst into something that was almost too much to bear. No—it wasn't an infatuation. He declared everlasting love. I had enjoyed every minute but didn't want him to cramp my style so it was easy for me to play the 'out of sight, out of mind' card. He on the other hand was more of the 'absence makes the heart grow fonder' school and while he wasted no time getting into the rhythm of London he made it quite clear that it was a question of 'when' and not 'if' we would meet again. Cocky so-and-so.

Truth was I couldn't get him out of my head and a few days

---

[9] Claude McLaren Reid 1902–1958.

later I invited him down again: to a fancy-dress party. I did take the precaution of asking my palmist, much fêted in society and known as The Great 'Cheiro' if this was wise; he gave me the 'all clear' and so without further ado ...

We carried on like this for most of February. Either him coming down to me or me going up to London where I could stay with Grandmama or Aunt Gladys. We went to shows, dined, danced and fitted in beautifully with the smart young blades and sixpences who surrounded us (we both called dangerously seductive or scheming women 'sixpences'). While not lacking enthusiasm, Harry's dancing skills were now so passé: he could just about manage a decent foxtrot but that was it. He needed educating. So I introduced him to jazz and all that went with it—ragtime, Jelly Roll Morton, the blues and all that American stuff that had yet to reach the Middle East.

We wrote to each other all the time. While I got my breath back in Brighton, he revelled in japes with his London house mates (I think he called them the 'chorus'), frequenting all kinds of low dives and partying with gay abandon. And, ever cautious, I retreated to the safety of Bonzo, who seemed to enjoy the emerging rivalry. Well, I may have thought I was being even-handed—after all I *was* kissing them both—but Harry's frustration just grew and grew:

> Is there any hope of Bonzo being sufficiently vamped up this weekend to make him lose all sense of proportion and fly into the arms of this temptress? If there is, I shall send him my heartiest congratulations, long life and prosperity; this is no misplaced sarcasm, I really would. I shall drink an aperitif to it tonight, perhaps two, who knows.
>
> HARRY TO ME, 18 FEBRUARY 1926

By now Harry had made it clear that, hell or high water, he was determined to marry me. He told others too and was really miffed when his sister tried to warn him off. What was I to do?

And *en passant*, while he denied it, I think he was somehow scared of the family and desperate for their approval.

> Darling, you are funny sometimes, why should I be scared of staying with your family. Nothing would scare me less, that is if I kept on the right side of them, which I sincerely hope I do. I should love to stay, then we can see lots and lots of each other, the more the better, don't you agree. Pity you are not staying with the family too because I usually feel very fit about breakfast time.
>
> HARRY TO ME, 17 FEBRUARY 1926

I did wonder sometimes if he had been in the East too long and didn't understand that we women had moved on from behaving like meek lambs and wanted to 'sing' as well.

> Margaret dear, what do you mean when you say you can't understand me and that it's like a great solid wall when you try to get a move on with me? Don't I get enough move on, or don't you understand the position between us?
>
> HARRY TO ME, 17 FEBRUARY 1926

And then he kept on about all the snakey women he encountered and his antics with the chorus. And he liked a bit of rough: dancing at 'low dancing halls' or the Junior Turf Club, where he could drink anything from coffee to Champagne at any time of the night, which suited him down to the ground.[10]

So, could I really take him seriously, and all his protestations

---

[10] The Junior Turf was one of several cabman's shelters in London. Many had nicknames, like the Bell and Horns at Thurloe Place in South Kensington or the Nursery End, near Lord's. The 'Junior' was outside Hyde Park Gate at Hyde Park Corner, said to be named after an invading clientele of aristocratic Champagne drinkers in the 1920s.

of love? I spent most of my time thinking I was just an amusement to him. Somehow Bonzo felt safer …

On top of this, Harry's brother Toby was beginning to pose a problem. He must have been about twenty-four and didn't really know what was what. He needed a job and big brother Harry felt obliged to jolly him along while he dithered about in search of something to get stuck into. Nice enough chap but increasingly burdensome. As far as Harry was concerned, caring for Toby in London while he wanted to be with me was a Bad Thing. But duty called and that was that. It still vexed him, as he kept on reminding me. But at least there were some humorous moments, particularly when Toby was vamped by young vixens who were too forward for him.

While this was all going on there was rather a lot of confusion about Harry's own future, once his leave was over. At some point he was going to be in London as some RAF bigshot's ADC. This, he thought, would get him promotion and (importantly) more money, which was always a 'big thing' with him—at least, the accumulating of it was; throughout his life he was far more reticent about spending it. The truth was that he had no other income. Ergo he couldn't marry me. Worse still, my family thought I could do much better for myself (i.e. by marrying Bonzo, who as you know was very well-heeled.)

Funnily enough this didn't bother me at the time; my allowance was more than Harry's salary and I could keep the two of us afloat. But it really irked him—and went on doing so for years and years.

> Margaret dear, I want to be engaged to you more than anything else,—I mean every word of this—but how can I? I am in a perpetual state of 'brokeness' which is far more annoying than you can ever imagine and it won't be repaired unless I get promoted or something else turns up.
>
> HARRY TO ME, 26 APRIL 1926

By now, what with jealousy getting well in the way and too much free time on his hands, Harry was sliding downhill. He came down for a couple of days in late April and struggled with what he saw as Bonzo's endless presence. His letters—ever ardent—grew morose. This began to grind me down.

> It is obvious that you can't love two people and if you love me as much as you say you do, why do you try to make me jealous of anybody else? And for you to find it hard to stop flirting with another man is the most peculiar form of love that I've ever come across. The reference to your lucky escape[11] was a beastly thing to say. I don't mind you going out with Bonzo but he will have to know which one you are in love with.
>
> HARRY TO ME, 18 APRIL 1926

I don't think it was just a question of keeping them both on a string. I finally came clean and to his utter dismay told him that I wasn't sure that he loved *me* enough, that I suspected he was a lifelong bachelor and that I was constraining his wish to fish in other ponds. I also feared that I would get in the way of his career. He was desperate. Angela didn't help either. She was convinced that he would chase anything in a skirt and was awash with warnings. Then she would tell me to stop fooling with him. (Little tramp: I knew she fancied him.)

All the same, it didn't stop him having a good time while he was on his own. And he was never slow to tell me all about it. I'm not sure why.

Around May we almost overboiled—there was just too much to cope with. On top of all this, protests by the miners had turned into the General Strike that began on 4 May and that caused widespread chaos. This forced the government to mob-

---

[11] Bonzo had not made me promise to give him up.

ilise troops to tackle the strikers and keep the buses and trains going. While some of Harry's fellow pilots had more glamorous jobs, such as flying mail from A to B, Harry had to settle for being a special constable. He spent his nights patrolling the docklands and getting increasingly frustrated because he didn't get the chance to thump anyone. And then, just to add to the fun, he came down with a pretty bad bout of flu—moaned like hell; not a model patient. Don't forget that it was not long since the influenza pandemic had killed off so many millions of people and although he didn't say he was worried, he grumbled a lot, leaving me very relieved when he began to mend.

In spite of muddles about where each of us might be at any time during the strike, we did manage to meet on a couple of occasions, and enjoyed ourselves—thankfully. Harry became more and more intense. We kissed so much that my chin got sore. He showered me with letters—often two or three times a week—trying his hardest not to lose me. He invited me to endless parties:

> I wish you would come darling—I'm not going to insist you do, so answer this as quickly as you can. I don't see any reason why you shouldn't except that you are so afraid of being talked about … Otherwise it is perfectly respectable. Margaret dear, I'm dying to see you again because I'm hopelessly in love with you and I am longing for the day that we may be able to be together—altogether.
>
> HARRY TO ME, 5 MAY 1926

At the same time he did his best to remind me that he too could play.

> I met a glorious snake the other night, tall dark and a wonderful figure—in fact a very striking-looking female and I have no doubt whatever that she likes being obliged,

but not by anybody. Don't you think I ought to introduce her to George[12] so that he could be seen about with somebody who is attractive, instead of that hay bag he trolls around with at present! You'll have to warn him however that she is expensive, but well worth it. We must always help our friends, Margaret. Don't misunderstand my appearance when you see me and think that I have been obliging here, there and everywhere!!! (It's only been here and there!)

HARRY TO ME, 17 MAY 1926

The toad! Thank heavens I was sufficiently confident of my own looks *not* to be threatened by this pomposity. As if our only purpose in life was to kowtow to over-entitled men and jump at their beck and call? He could be bloody rude as well; describing one photograph that I gave him as 'purely a study in hairdressing' (nothing wrong with my beautiful 'shingle' which, as it happened, was at the height of fashion).

Eventually I realised that there were two things going on here. Firstly, retaliation when I told him of my own misbehaviour. Secondly, he had a deep conviction that beauty (in women, at least) was to be noticed and admired; so commentary on this or that beauty was perhaps not to be taken as a threat but as appreciation. The nasty side of this was that he could be horribly critical of those women whose looks did not please him; unbelievably unkind. I'm not saying that this reduced my irritation sometimes, but I did begin to understand him. Fortunately my own self-confidence in this regard kept me sane.

So what was I supposed to do? Attempting to gain some perspective I concluded that my life otherwise was easy; the team at Hove did a good job looking after David, I had plenty of money and the style to go with it and had grown immune to

---

[12] Another George, not Bonzo.

people telling me that it was high time for me to find another husband. Alongside this, Angela was a good pal. We spent ages together hunting for clothes, learning new dance moves and swapping stories (but not men). Luckily, we both had good legs and revelled in hem lines that kept moving further upwards. I even wondered whether to take up the invitations that we still received to be mannequins and model clothes (Harry was very curious about this).

Thinking further, although terrified of attracting gossip I could come and go as I pleased. Yes, I was playing safe. No, I shouldn't have been jumping from one pair of arms to another. Yes, I did think about marrying Harry. And Bonzo too. I tried to be honest with them both but didn't make a very good job of it. Trouble was, I fancied them both, struggling like hell not to jump into bed with them. At one point Harry was convinced that I wanted to ditch him, to get him to forget me and release me to Bonzo.

And then relief—of sorts. Well, a breather anyway. Having given the ADC job to someone else, the RAF decided to send Harry off to a place called Upavon, some twenty miles north of Salisbury. And—hurrah!—he had plenty to take his mind off things and some calm descended. He cheered up too.

He continued to shower me with loving letters (Bonzo couldn't touch him in that department) and in that way managed to survive most of June without me. If anything, he became a bit of a schemer. To my surprise and relief (or deep suspicion) he continued to be polite to Bonzo and even tried to socialise with him from time to time; talk about getting to know your enemy! Also I think he was more relaxed about his brother Toby, who was now about to sail off to Malaya and become a customs officer. We all met at the end of the month near Hampton Court for a jolly party to see Toby off. Very romantic—moonlight by the river, and all that. And why did Harry have to be so adorable … ?

Harry's stint at Upavon meandered into July. He thrived on

a diet of flying, dancing, tennis, shooting and adventures in the Wiltshire countryside—invariably with pretty women. And—still *sans* car—he didn't think twice about 'borrowing' an aeroplane if he wanted to visit someone. He even came close to learning how to tango. At some point he went up to the Palace to receive his DFC. They (the RAF) were obviously pleased with his flying and even let him wriggle out of any written exams. Lucky fellow: he could charm the birds out of the trees … .

But it didn't last. Halfway through July he learned that he was to go to somewhere near Chester as an instructor. I'm not sure who was the more galled: him or me. It really put the skids on our seeing each other. It began as 'a month or so' and stretched into three … . One thing that did help, though, was that the pressure to sleep with him faded, in my mind at least. True, it had been hard not to, but I was still hung up about appearances and my mind was somewhat stuck. But Chester! It was miles away and just as our relationship was really beginning to click, he was gone. What was I to do—head off to a nunnery? I'm not sure whether I was just angry or hurt: probably a bit of both … .

Harry hated Chester and went on bombarding me with letters. In a funny way he couldn't help mixing his loneliness from me and his attempts at local mischief. He even sent me photos and an extraordinary list of mystifying captions. Some were of his family, but others were of me but also various past girlfriends. The only saving grace was that he marked me as 'best of the bunch' or something like that. Very cheeky.

Bonzo and I continued to see each other. Well of course we did. I remember him clowning around with me and Angela at the West Worthing tennis tournament in August and the three of us agreed to join a party of friends heading for Tremezzo, a little town on the western shores of Lake Como the following month. Harry tried to shrug this off but I knew he was hurt.

Harry in the doldrums

Harry spent three weeks undergoing an intensive course at Upavon, flying AVRO 504s and refreshing the flying instructor skills he had developed early on in his career. Having satisfied his assessors and generally enjoyed himself in June, he then expected to be sent to the RAF Cadet College at Cranwell but the move was postponed and on 19 July 1926 he transferred instead to RAF Sealand—officially No. 5 Flying Training School—which he nicknamed 'Fighting Training School'.

Once he got there, he was horrified to find he might have to stay for three years, which felt like a prison sentence. Nothing was right about the place; marooned about seven miles west of Chester, he thought it a great disappointment. More to the point, it was 250 miles from Hove and me. He was desperate to get away, and returning to Upavon seemed like his best option.

Money worries now featured more and more in his letters to me, along with intense frustration that he had little or no control over what I was up to, poor dear, particularly as I was to spend most of September with Bonzo in Italy. To add to his misery and confusion, I have to admit that I started teasing him about his previous girlfriends and even accused him (falsely, of course) of confusing me with one of them. (How could he possibly?!) At the same time my dalliance with Bonzo continued along with my flirtations with various others that Harry considered unworthy competitors.

But to his credit, his ardour and determination stood firm. Along with frustration, retaliation and the occasional dollop of sarcasm, his letters expressed longing and devotion, along with a reluctant acceptance of my independence.

> Darling, I wish I could have seen you in your jade green dress and hat at Goodwood—you must have been extremely easy to look at. ... Perhaps owing to all the training I have

had from you I might have said quite a lot and made you blush delightfully!

HARRY TO ME, 23 AUGUST 1926

I didn't make it easy for him. One minute I would confess to one misdeed or another, the next I would sweetly offer to knit him a sweater (which I did and which he loved). Privately I was tormented with worry over my son's continued ill-health, which led to a minor operation in August. It didn't help that his medical care was in the hands of Dr Seymour, a colleague of my father's and an old family friend. This made me a little uncomfortable: was his knowledge really up to date?

There was a certain 'don't mess with me' streak in Harry's letters. He would retaliate against my provocations and jibes with threats to pursue this or that pretty young thing he had met or tales of expeditions to the 'happy hunting grounds of Wallasey', where birds of all feathers flocked together.

Nevertheless he willingly gave me advice on which night clubs in London to try and how to find them, and of course he wanted to know how I got on—a sign of growing confidence, perhaps? Otherwise he busied himself with tennis, cricket, shooting (for free), dancing, dinners and the occasional show in Liverpool.

> Fulford and I and two females went to see *The Student Prince* in Liverpool last Thursday. It was a very good show. We then took the first bint home where we chatted and had light refreshments for a short time and then did the same with the second one. She gave me some lessons in the Charleston and I think I can now do it without having to think about my feet the whole time, so the next time we dance we ought to be able to manage it—are you an expert at it now?
>
> HARRY TO ME, 21 SEPTEMBER 1926

It would have helped if Harry had been happier in his work but he found that flying instruction presented difficulties and frustrations of its own. Everyone at Sealand had to wear parachutes when flying, which for someone as tall as Harry was worrying; as the instructor in training aircraft with dual controls where the trainee sat in the seat behind, would there be enough room in the front seat for him to get out quickly?

As it was there were several crashes, one fatal. And once, when Harry's aircraft's engine suddenly stopped when quite close to the ground, it required all his flying skill to bounce the machine safely over a rather solid fence and land on the other side. I know this because, for a change, he chose to tell me all about it, having always made great efforts *not* to relate such events to his mother for fear of them getting back to me. I was horrified at the thought that he might have died—and maybe that was why he mentioned it.

Meanwhile, in the background, he applied steady but gentle pressure on the powers-that-be to manoeuvre a return south.

I travelled to Italy at the beginning of September for the long-planned two-week holiday. This brought something of a truce after August, during which I had rather fiercely put a stopper on Harry's staying with my parents and thereby of his seeing me that month. But his ardour stayed firm and he refused to be put off by my tales of the various men I was dating in London. He seemed confident that I would stick with him in the end. Perhaps he realised I was testing him—or testing myself—before making any final decision.

After a gap of some ten weeks we finally met, over the last weekend in September. This must have served as a wake-up call for us both as, in spite of some fierce quarrels, we emerged as a stronger couple and the postal sniping ceased. Friends who met us passed the word around, and the Hove gossip machine began to turn. We had managed to find ourselves—or maybe we had matured: was the Bonzo threat now over?

Shortly afterwards, Harry's persistence paid off: he was to instruct at the RAF's officer training establishment at Cranwell in Lincolnshire and moved there on 12 October. Although this only brought him fifty miles closer to me, he was far more positive about the new job and the place that went with it.

It took him a whole month to arrange for me to visit Cranwell and for us to see each other. For one thing there was the vexed question of female accommodation. Harry reluctantly went along with my continued preoccupation with appearances, finding a hotel room for me while he slept at the station (at heart, in spite of bombing unruly tribesmen, he was an honourable man). Once he had managed that, and been persuaded that it would be difficult for me to bring my sister with me (what was I thinking of?), I obviously made a favourable impression on those of his colleagues who met us while we did the rounds of Cranwell together.

By now our thoughts on marriage had shifted from 'perhaps' to 'when'. As well as briefing his sceptical sister, Harry even wrote to his mother in Florence to warn her of this possibility. He was rewarded with a summons to Italy to tell her all about it face to face.

Fortunately, opinion at Hove seemed to be inching in our favour. Reluctantly or not, and in spite of Harry's impecunity, my parents were delighted to find me looking happy and well. Reading a report in the local press about my prowess on the dance floor, Harry was promoted to remark:

> So, I am going to marry one of Brighton's dancing "fans" am I? I like the way they say all kinds of nice things about you at the beginning of the article. …
>
> HARRY TO ME, 20 NOVEMBER 1926

And at last David's health improved.

Harry fitted in easily at Cranwell and its grand surroundings. His pupils did well, he got on fine with his CO and he complied with the various administrative and social demands that came his way. He also had a highly unusual office clerk:

> We are very sad in our flight as we are losing the inimitable Colonel Lawrence who is the office clerk. He makes an excellent clerk and we are not likely to get another as good. I would back him against anybody at making a fire without any wood. His £30 book[13] will be published very soon now. I want to have a look at an original one if I can get it out of him but it needs very careful handling. It's strange to think that he could have been Governor of Iraq, Palestine or Egypt if he had wanted to, instead of hiding himself as he does.
>
> HARRY TO ME 27 OCT 1926

Flying however has never been without its risks. Harry told me that he had watched as one pupil pilot flying below him slammed his aircraft into the ground after a vertical fall of about 300ft and, having landed swiftly to 'help with the corpse', was astounded to find that, against all odds, the pilot had escaped from the wreckage unhurt.

Not every pupil was as fortunate; a couple of weeks later another died in a serious crash. At a time when machine faults were not unusual, there was general relief that this accident was the result of pilot error (he had failed to come out of a spin) rather than a duff aircraft.

Harry himself had the occasional prang. On one occasion he 'very nearly turned the machine on its back' but escaped injury.

---

[13] *The Seven Pillars of Wisdom.*

Off the station he made friends, explored East Anglia, took up beagling and enjoyed the shooting season; he even managed to bag the odd snipe or two—no mean feat. But then he *was* an excellent shot.

By the time I reached Italy I was exhausted. True, I had been having a rather wild time but I had been worrying myself sick about David. Fortunately, Daddy was confident that he and Dr Seymour understood what was wrong and how to deal with it; but why had he been ill for so long? And my feelings were very mixed up about Harry.

I had to sort my thoughts out and now was the time to do it. My grand decision was to give Harry the benefit of the doubt and believe that he really did love me. Yes, he could carp and yes, he did have a habit of retaliating when things didn't go his way. He was also unnecessarily obsessive about silly things but there was something rather convincing about him. Aside from our squabbles he was wonderful company—devoted, handsome, brave, vital and persuasive. A wonderful kisser, too: Bonzo didn't even come close, not least because we also used to have blazing rows (which continued when he joined our little party in the lakes for a few days). Yes, I concluded: the scorecard was weighted firmly in Harry's favour.

So perhaps it was time to stop worrying about what the family might think, or whether we were the perfect couple, or whether other contenders had more to offer me, or whether Harry in turn would always be tempted by the next young thing, or whether, indeed, I might get hurt if either of us chose wrongly. The thing is that part of me kept thinking that I was young and fun, and that other young people were 'fun', and that young people have a once-in-a-lifetime chance to have fun, and that turning your back on fun marks you down as old and dull. But another part of me was thinking that fun couldn't go on forever, and perhaps it was time to buckle down and face the music.

That is what I was thinking when Harry and I eventually met at Hove near the end of September. I think I wanted to put all my qualms away and be more mature but, to his frustration, I found I still couldn't quite believe that he wanted us to get engaged. I was sure there was a catch somewhere … .

The next couple of months were something of a whirlwind. Harry moved to Cranwell and I began to believe in us, as I realised more and more how much we had in common: our style, our humour, our fashion likes, our taste in food and cocktails—and fancying each other rotten. We trod a good measure on the dance floor (even if his Charleston was dreadful) and thrived at parties. He had energy, and if it was fun I was after—and evidently it was—fun is what he was. Sensual too. I thought that these pluses outweighed the minuses of his having no money and my parents' being unconvinced.

I spent two very happy weekends with Harry at Cranwell. We let ourselves think about marriage, although the idea of having to wait two years or so before he got a promotion was galling. And of course there was the small matter of persuading Daddy that Harry, albeit poor, was suitable.

I did rather enjoy a little game I played. I told David what I wanted to do and he seized on the idea of having a sister. So we invented one and called her Harriet. This completely foxed Harry for a while:

> Talking of 'Harriet' (horrible name) I should also hate her to announce her arrival too soon—I think I should emigrate if she did! … Won't David be disappointed though when he finds out that she is a myth!
> HARRY TO ME, 26 NOVEMBER 1926

Somehow the idea of living with Harry at Cranwell seemed to fit, although his tales of flying prangs put the fear of God into me. The RAF chaps even asked him to provide a dental chart so that he could be recognised if burnt. Horrid … .

To make up for the long separations we wrote each other frequent letters, which were now much more peaceful. It was a relief to be able to tell Harry how much I cared for him and missed him. I began what became a long tradition of sending each other earthy jokes, which he gallantly called 'stories'. He was convinced that women knew all the best ones and he delighted in passing them on to his mess mates.

At some point his sister Sylvia invited him to join her in December in Florence, where she and their mother Alice had lived for a while. This was probably more of an instruction than a request but as Harry hadn't seen either of them for over four years and he wanted their thoughts on 'me', he felt duty bound to comply.

And so off to Italy he went, happy. As for Bonzo, he had been consigned to history. At least, so we both thought ... .

Harry in Italy

A fortnight before the end of the year, Harry left England for what turned out to be the better part of six weeks. After an uneventful train journey via Paris, he reached Florence and was embraced by his mother and sister.

As I later learned, Alice Reid—ever a staunch Scot—was thoroughly cosmopolitan. Following her husband's death, she had resolved that her young daughter should be equally outward-looking and that she should complete her schooling on the Continent. So, freed of any ties to England, she settled in Florence and bought the Italian equivalent of a town house. Via Proconsul 10 proved ideal. Hidden in a narrow street but close to the city centre there was plenty of space for her and Sylvia, whom she installed in what she called her 'top floor flat', after leaving finishing school in France.

Harry was surprised and enchanted. To begin with, at least, he found his mother in fine fettle; as for Sylvia, she astounded him. Not only had she blossomed into an attractive young woman but, having finished her schooling at an exclusive establishment in Florence (where she excelled at painting), she now knew her way around the city and knew who was who and what was what. Who better to show him around?

The weeks that followed might have taken a very different turn, had Harry not already committed himself to me. The city was awash with temptation: he had never come across so many beautiful women. At the same time, he was enraptured by the place and quietly determined that this was where he and I should honeymoon—an interesting way of turning its delights around in his mind.

He bombarded—no, cascaded—me with loving letters. Most people can fit 'I love you' or some such into a few words; but Harry could fill whole pages with endearments, which I found very touching. That doesn't mean that he shirked from describing his social life and its many encounters. It was probably just as well that Sylvia accompanied him for much of this time—chaperoning him, in reverse, you might say.

As instructed, Harry wasted no time in tackling his mother about me, his determination to marry me and my suitability. He need not have worried. He had come armed with some very convincing photographs and amused both his mother and Sylvia with his various descriptions and tales.

> I told her how well you run your household and how you make your own dresses (some of them!). She loves the jumper too, I think she is prepared to like you very much and of course she won't be able to help it when she sees you, will she?
>
> HARRY TO ME, 18 DECEMBER 1926

Sylvia proved to be a capable guide, culturally and socially. But having done his best to soak up the various galleries and palaces to which she led him, he gave up; 'I don't think I will be able to stand much more of it, besides they are as cold as charity inside'. He preferred to sit out the middle of the day at a bar called Doneys, where the cocktails were excellent and there was plenty to watch and enjoy:

> I remember you once told me how embarrassed Angela used to be at looking at statues with fig leaves—you can tell her that Florence would be the ideal place for her as only 1% wear them here—they don't seem to have ever been in fashion.
>
> HARRY TO ME, 22 DECEMBER 1926

His blandishments continued to produce results.

> Yesterday, Sylvia volunteered the remark that she thought you must be very nice. If she says anything like that, she must think quite a lot of you as she is very sparing with compliments and not easily pleased. I've told my family you have a cocktail voice … don't jump out of your chair with rage—even if you hate having it called a cocktail voice, I love it—the voice, I mean, not the name, although I like that too.
>
> HARRY TO ME, 24 DECEMBER 1926

While succeeding in Florence, he only wished that Daddy was as easy to convince back in Hove; what with his alarmist views on pilots and their 'inevitably short life spans', he remained an obstacle. Just as well that Mama was on Harry's side.

> I hope you don't get worried about me breaking my neck [while flying] because I don't intend to if I can possibly help it … Talk your father round sweetheart because I don't want him to be an obstructionist. Longing to be with you again.
>
> HARRY TO ME, 27 DECEMBER 1926

Do you know what really terrified him? I started to have driving lessons. He wondered why on Earth I had chosen winter time to start and whether I would resist the temptation to copy [my friend] Shelagh's mad antics on the road? And would I please not follow my mother's 'bad habit of taking corners at 50 mph'.

> Yes darlingest, do learn to drive the car but I hope you won't be as dangerous as Sheelah is—I don't want that adorable neck of yours broken, Sheelah is bound to break hers sooner or later.
>
> HARRY TO ME, 24 DECEMBER 1926

Sylvia continued to amaze him. He had barely recognised the eighteen-year-old when they met. She was pretty, with shingled hair, and didn't need makeup or scent; she dressed well and was confident and socially at ease. She was also an accomplished horsewoman. She had landed a plum job doing French and Italian translation for the American consul and shared a big office with a baroness, finding plenty of opportunity for long lunches and midday visits to Florence's many art collections (she would eventually become an accomplished portrait painter and sculptor). On the minus side, Harry was distressed by Sylvia's ability to flare up in a temper over very little.

Harry relished his time in Florence and the surrounding countryside. He delighted in the charm of the buildings, the range and quality of beautiful goods in the shops (particularly the clothes, which he knew would entrance me) and the overall way of life. He certainly thought that the Italians drank far less than most, particularly the Americans. As for food, on the other hand … .

For some reason he concluded that it was the most moral city he had ever been in, noting that 'only one female has made cow's eyes—I mean sheep's eyes—at me in the street. Business must be very poor in that direction'. Cow's eyes, sheep's eyes, my eye! Knowing him, his vanity must have been pricked by this only happening once!

But heavens, he was spoilt. Sylvia introduced him widely and he shortly built up an impressive network of friends. He dined and danced prolifically, making the most of the lavish entertainments at Christmas and the New Year:

> Last night was great fun and we didn't get back until 4.30 this morning. As we were an odd number, I had to do something about it, so I introduced myself to an English female with an attractive girl. At first, she checked me over for a second and then burst out into a grin, luckily for me. After that I left my party and had a very good time! They seemed to know most people so I got introduced to one or two very nice young things. When I apologised for introducing myself, she said 'for heaven's sake don't speak so loudly, most people understand English'—it quite frightened the poor thing. I had a bit of bad luck though: there was an absolutely stunning girl in one party and I had got [the English girl] to promise to introduce us but the end came and it couldn't be done.
>
> HARRY TO ME, 1 JANUARY 1927

Mercifully, Harry wrote almost every day, and I was comforted that despite all this—the discoveries, jollity and enjoyment with his family—he really missed me. He had time to reflect: apart from the physical and emotional excitement side of things, we had survived the roller-coaster and trauma of the past year; having found that we could achieve happiness together, he was anxious now not to lose that. Even a day without a letter from me upset him, and some of his insecurities lingered. For one thing he wished Bonzo would do the decent thing and just vanish. Even I was confused: was

Bonzo's presence at weekends in Brighton simply friendly or did he still hope for another chance? Or was he now more interested in Angela?

> No my beautiful darling I don't mind you going to London with Bonzo because I think the only one you care two hoots about is myself—If I thought differently it would be quite another story, or if I thought you would flirt with him I would be furious and there would be a rumpus such as Bonzo has been expecting but I hope will never take place.
> HARRY TO ME, 29 DECEMBER 1926

But, deep down, I did wonder if Bonzo's ghost was rattling him a little.

> I still find it beastly difficult to get to sleep at night just through thinking of you, so I have to put the light on again and read for hours. Then I imagine myself in Somaliland chasing the nimble lion and eventually pass out—it's becoming quite a habit now. I don't see any cure for it until we are together. ... I'm so glad you are getting masses of wonderful underclothes, darlingest (somehow it doesn't seem right me saying this) but you should see the underclothes to be got in Florence—they would make a witch look beautiful. I think we ought to come to Florence for our honeymoon and collect some much nicer things than one can get in England.
> HARRY TO ME, 4 JANUARY 1927

Some of his letters made me hoot with laughter. He was good at mixing humour with more serious thoughts.

> Margaret darling, if you love me as much as I love you, we are going to have a marvellous married life.

Darlingest, I got off with a girl in Doney's this morning with a glass eye—I mean that she had a glass eye!!! Sounds as if I am losing my sense of proportion doesn't it!! Pray for me sweetheart will you, in case I get off with one who has a wooden leg!! Splinters are beastly things. ...

One of mother's reasons for liking you is that you look a sensible girl—she can't stand the empty-headed type. Sylvia first started liking you when she saw the jumper that you had knitted for me, she rather admires you for being able to do it because she couldn't.

HARRY TO ME 6 JANUARY 1927

Then, half-way into January, the sybaritic calm collapsed. Alice was found unconscious. She was taken to hospital where, revived by gulps of oxygen, she made slow progress. She was well nursed and after a couple of weeks, to the relief of all, was 'strong enough to have a good row'. Harry and Sylvia spent hours at her bedside.

While all this was going on in Italy, I had to cope with one or two worries at home.

For one thing, the saga of Bonzo and Angela was becoming extremely tiresome. Angela was playing Bonzo off against another George, couldn't make up her mind which of them to turn to first, and even holidayed in Switzerland with them both. She asked me for my advice and then, when I gave it, I was caught in the crossfire and got all sorts of flak from her.

The other had to do with David. The poor lad had developed an abscess on his back that turned septic. It took about three weeks of surgery and other care to deal with and there were times when my faith in Dr Seymour wavered. Would the boy ever be truly well again? Harry was very concerned, and did not understand my reluctance to tell him the whole story.

At the same time, we ached to see each other:

My darlingest darling. I can't call you anything more loving than this, although I should like to because I feel very very loving. I just want to be with you and smother you with kisses.

'Won't it be lovely darling just sitting on that sofa of yours again while I tell you all that I've been doing since I have been here …

HARRY TO ME, 23 JANUARY 1927

Just as I was beginning to relax, my old friend Muriel got a job as a mannequin. Harry must have thought I was tempted to follow suit, and was quick to lay down the law.

The other question about mannequins. No, I'd hate you to be one, at least I think I would! I don't want to think about you parading yourself in front of heaps of people especially when I'm not there!

HARRY TO ME, 27 JANUARY 1927

Once Alice was back at home, things in Florence settled and Harry was able to busy himself with preparations for his return. He bought lots of presents. 'What Houbigant[14] do you like best,' he wrote: '*Le Parfum Ideal, Quelques Fleurs* or what?'

Farewells made, he was free to go home. He had written an impressive thirty-one letters to me but still received the occasional rocket from me for not managing to write every day. (To be fair, nor did I.)

---

[14] Houbigant is a Parisian perfume house, founded in 1775 by Jean-François Houbigant. It became a favoured brand of fragrance, patronised by royalty, from Marie Antoinette to Queen Victoria.

ROYAL AIR FORCE,
CRANWELL,
SLEAFORD, LINCS.

6 · 12 · 26.

Darlingest Margaret.

I missed the post again yesterday morning. I suppose you will blow me up for it - more better not though as the last one didn't arrive!! I was out on Saturday evening and so tired

Chapter 9
The Big Leap

> Got hold of an aeroplane after being called at 4.15
> and then set off northwards with Padre Jagoe in the
> back. We got right above the clouds at 15,000 ft and
> had a wonderful view, but we got as cold as a frog in
> an icebound pool. ... As soon as it was over I pointed
> the nose to earth and came down like a bat out of hell
> through the clouds and then found I didn't know
> where I was, so had to land in a field and ask a yokel
> where we were ...
> HARRY TO ME, 29 JUNE 1927

Harry came back at the beginning of February. Goodness, we were so relieved to be together again in what was a truly joyful reunion—so much so that after almost exactly a year we finally slept together—my first time since Horace. Not fair to make comparisons, but impossible to ignore Harry's drive and energy. Then, after a wonderful weekend, he returned to Cranwell and two weeks later came to London to be with me again. This at last set the scene and we settled down to a workable routine. We *would* marry and, decision made, all was suddenly (relatively) quiet. It was a great relief. And very strange.

Now the drama moved to the old folk. In Hove, after only four or five years at Brunswick Square, the aged relatives had somehow managed to agree to move on from elegant grandeur to something more practical *and* a real garden. They chose a substantial Edwardian pile at the top of Furze Hill called Helouan, less than a mile from me at Wilbury Crescent.

David seemed to be on the mend as well, which was also comforting. After about three months the surgery to remove and clean out his skin abscess seemed to have worked and the wound on his back was free of pus. And yet, as the weeks passed, he was still unwell. I tried to persuade myself that it was nothing serious but found it harder and harder. Harry did his best to reassure me that it would all turn out alright, but his words were not enough.

At the end of February Harry and I had our first dirty weekend—at a London hotel. The occasion was a Royal Navy ball at Greenwich, courtesy of brother Nick. The dance was great fun—all those fancy RN uniforms. Harry was very proud of me, relishing endless admiring glances from the others. Our time together afterwards was idyllic. As far as he was concerned, the only thing that prevented us from marrying soon was lack of cash. He had recently taken his promotion exams and the thought of a pay rise had spurred him on to some fairly serious revision.

There was just one fly in the ointment: blasted Bonzo just wouldn't go away. Worse than that, I couldn't work out what he was really after, unless he was fishing for Angela (in which case he had an odd way of going about it). It drove Harry mad; made him curious as well:

> 'I think Bonzo must just have wanted a flirtation to begin with … and most of it was trying to make you jealous when he was in Brighton. He probably hoped that you would then find you liked him more than me'.
>
> HARRY TO ME, 15 FEBRUARY 1926

Well, you could say we had some drama of our own. One of Harry's stories went something like this: 'Do you know the difference between delight and a fright? A month!' Well, no sooner had he written this than it was my turn to have a *real* fright. Somewhere around Easter I realised I was late and I panicked; something must have gone wrong with the 'protection' during our last meeting in London.

Harry wrote frantically to allay my fears, doing his best to reassure me that I couldn't possibly be pregnant because he had worn two French letters and was sure that neither, let alone both, had broken. I explored all options and—to Harry's horror—was tempted by all manner of pills that might resolve a problem that might or might not exist. Bless him: he even consulted the Cranwell quack, who explained that such events were not unusual, particularly if I was nervous about things (well, there had been a three-year gap and Harry's 'size' was, shall we say, rather alarming at our first encounter.)

With great trepidation I confided in Dr Seymour, on whom I had relied for David's diagnosis and treatment (looking back, hardly a similar complaint). He also did his best to reassure, telling me that a delay of one or two weeks was not at all unusual and prescribing me something to calm me down.

After about two weeks of misery and nightmares, the fright proved to be phony. Clear thought returned and I calmed down. But aside from the relief, the fear that I *might* get pregnant before our wedding called a halt to any further adventures—regardless of Harry's dismay; he would just have to keep his distance until we had reached the aisle.

Fortunately, these events didn't bring everything else to a grinding halt and somewhere around the middle of March I managed to jerk Harry from his beagling and boxing (would you believe) and get him to think about announcing our engagement. I suppose I did accept his protestations—that this couldn't happen until he had given me a ring—were fair enough and eventually he commissioned his mother to have a ring made for me—in Florence!—providing a detailed specification for the setting.[1]

---

[1] Sapphire in the centre, ringed with four diamonds and four sapphires.

Just as Harry had agreed that we should simply get on with it rather than wait for the ring, he learned that protocol required him to get his CO's permission before any announcement could be made. While this prompted furious but unnecessary plotting (how, where and when?), in the event his CO greeted his request with delight, offered his congratulations and his blessing—and that was that. All that had to be done now was to negotiate the wording and Daddy could fire the thing off. Thus, on 28 March, the *Times* declared:

The engagement is announced between Harry REDVERS MCLAREN REID D.F.C., RAF, elder son of the late Mr H. Reid, of Buenos Aires, and Mrs Reid, of Florence, Italy and MARGARET, widow of Maj. H.A. Goldsmith M.C., IA and elder daughter of Dr and Mrs Copeman, of Hove, Sussex.

Suddenly we had things to plan—the wedding and where to live for a start. Who would have thought it would take seven months to pull it all together?

We still lived apart and our meetings were never long or frequent enough. Harry's social life at Cranwell seemed to mushroom and he tried all manner of tricks to get me up to Lincolnshire to join in. When I did, and bowled him over with some stunning new dresses, he gave me a real rocket for wearing too much warpaint on one occasion when we stayed with the padre.

I remember coming away from Cranwell freshly aware of two things. Firstly, that I would now be on the spot, as it were, at those moments when news came of an instructor or a cadet crashing an aircraft (frightening). Secondly, I did begin to get a feel for what it might be like to live there, and sensed, happily, that I might survive. I even toyed with the idea of living in married quarters.

And, to David's delight, Harry had bought a puppy cocker

spaniel and wanted me to name it. When I prevaricated, he took matters into his own hands and christened the pup 'Zakho' after his famously uncomfortable stint in northern Iraq.

Meanwhile I flitted between Hove and London. There was plenty to do. And I was more and more curious about Angela and Bonzo: 'were they' or 'weren't they'? (Ominously, it seemed as though Bonzo was playing her off against another young thing.)

And so the spring came and went. While Harry was busy flying and organising the cadets' gym and what have you, his sports responsibilities took him further and further afield, with cricket matches every weekend. His game got better; my tennis, on the other hand, continued to slide.

Around this time Cranwell was in the spotlight because of an attempt to fly a Hawker biplane non-stop to Karachi. After various failed attempts and witnessed by thousands, the plane

Harry (front row, second from right) with his cricketing pals, in flannels.

got off the ground safely—much to Harry's relief, in view of the half-ton or so of extra fuel that it carried. Unfortunately, or so I heard, the crew was forced to ditch in the Persian Gulf, having flown non-stop for almost thirty-five hours and over 3,400 miles. This remarkable achievement was enough to qualify them as holders of the record for non-stop flying—but only for one day, before being pipped by Lindbergh's triumphant Atlantic crossing. A second, unsuccessful attempt a few weeks later almost ended in disaster.

June began badly. I had decided to join Harry for a fleeting visit to London rather than accept an invitation to the Derby at Epsom. For no fault of his own, he couldn't get away on the day and I ended up rattling around my grandmother's house in London. We were both sore about this, particularly as we were unlikely to meet again for several weeks.

Our letters now changed gear. Yes, Harry still regaled me with tales of endless entertainment but now came serious domestic discussion alongside his many passionate entreaties. He found a little house to rent which we both agreed was preferable to what he called 'Harmony Row' on the station. It was not far from Cranwell and needed furnishing, but that was doable. To my amusement, this was the moment he had to admit that I knew much more about this sort of thing than he did, which gave me plenty to contribute; he even left most of the summer-holiday planning to me. Then out of the blue, Alice offered to loan us her flat, which finally decided us to honeymoon in Florence, as Harry had wanted, rather than in France.

After a blissful weekend at the end of June we were apart for a whole month and did our best not to be miserable about it. There was however something to celebrate: Harry was promoted to flight lieutenant. Although he was in something of a blue funk because of the exams he had to pass, over the course of a week, to qualify for the next rung up when he had returned from Italy, he had obviously got through. That meant a little more income, which cheered him up no end. The only snag was that he feared he might be posted elsewhere as he hadn't been trained to run the gym and his CO wanted someone who had. In the event this was an unnecessary scare.

In the meantime I made myself busy looking after David, enjoying summer entertainments, hunting for clothes and trying to buy a car. But my attempts at calm were shattered by another fright. My attempts to stay chaste until our wedding day had failed and I was late again. In panic, I resorted to pills, without any clear medical logic. Harry was appalled and did his best to reassure and guide me with daily letters, and to persuade me to ditch Dr Seymour, the faithful family retainer and friend, who was now definitely too close for comfort, as far as gossip was concerned. After a more balanced encounter with a London doctor and a week of more misery, normality returned and my anticipated shame melted away. Phew …

It must have been around this time that I decided that his pecker needed a name. He was so damn proud of it that I christened it 'Wilfred'—a nickname that stuck forever. Unfortunately, baptising it was kept firmly at bay until we had emerged from the wedding chapel.

Harry in the meantime was busy with endless guest nights: back-to-back sports (cricket, tennis and boxing), attempting to keep the cadets fit, and flying. The idiot even managed to break his nose while showing off in the gym. (I ran a poor third in the sympathy stakes.)

I was still in two minds about the flying. I knew that Harry was an excellent pilot and was very happy in the air but the dread that he might suffer the same fate as several of his friends who crashed to their death never left me.

At last the month apart was over and I went up to Cranwell to join Harry for the Cadets' Ball, which was a great success. What's more, after a couple of days there and an inspection of the house (rather sweet), I was less uneasy about the prospect of living there.

We (that is, us and the puppy) managed to stay in London for a couple of days, then motored down to Buxted in East Sussex, where I had hired a room, and began an idyllic couple of weeks on our own—the longest period we had yet spent together. Add in a few duty visits to Hove and elsewhere and it ended up totalling a month of holiday. We even got Angela to confess about her goings on with Bonzo, which seemed to be going somewhere at last—hoorah! Somehow we managed to stay calm while Mama fussed over wedding minutiae and Harry returned to work, refreshed and happy—as was I. There were one or two loose ends to tie up and we had the whole of September to do that. Number one on the list (his list) was 'rubberwear'. Typical man: he left it all up to me:

> I think the best thing to do about the various little 'rubber goods' would be for you to write a note to Heppell's and tell them to send you the things. I don't look forward to going and asking for them myself. You can also get them to send the various 'tonics' whatever they are. It would be an awful shame to spoil our first night for lack of such etceteras methinks!
>
> HARRY TO ME, 12 SEPTEMBER 1927

At least there was one thing that didn't require debate; rather it erred on an instruction. Somewhere along the line (it must have been when I was in Mespot) Daddy decided to invest his ill-gotten gains in two Brighton seafront hotels. This got him a seat on their boards, which fitted in nicely with his thirst for being one of the town's movers and shakers. One, the Old Ship, was built on the site of the Old Ship Inn by a chap called Tattersall, who had earned his wealth as a sea captain by ferrying Charles II from Brighton to France and safety in 1651 when on the run from Cromwell.

But the Old Ship didn't fit for our wedding. No. Daddy was in no doubt where we should hold the reception: his second

Harry and me at Helouan, August 1927. It's a very awkward pose.

investment was in the Bedford, widely regarded as the most distinguished late-Georgian building in Brighton after the Royal Pavilion. It was the town's leading hotel for the accommodation of royalty, the fashionable and the famous. Charles Dickens had stayed there. So—no contest. For once it was easy to do what we were told.

Around this time Harry had begun calling me 'Peg' or

'Peggy' again. Yes, it was a recognised nickname for Margaret but it reminded me of my childhood. It took me a while to persuade him that, much as he might like the name, I did not.

While I worked through the finer points of wedding planning, Harry wrestled with the landlord of the house over various repairs, and dealt with furnishings. He even managed to appoint a maid. Nothing, however, managed to deflect him from the new shooting season, and braces of pheasant and partridge made their way down to Hove with very tasty frequency.

Bar very rare phone calls, all admin and decision-making had to be done by post: would we like this or that wedding present? Have you written to thank them? Should we invite X? Will this furniture 'do'? Who should watch over the house while we are away? Is the car ready yet? It was endless. Unsurprisingly, darling Harry left it to me to find presents for the bridesmaids.

We had endless discussions about clothes, including my wedding dress. Harry had very clear ideas about male dress but while he had strong views on what might or might not look good on me, was not remotely *au fait* with the vocabulary of female attire when I wrote to him with suggestions. Still, we did manage to find moments of light relief:

> You quite frightened me when you said you would have a rehearsal with Heppell's goods!!! I thought you expressed it so badly that it might mean you thought of securing the services of some attractive young man with whom to try it out!!!!!
>
> HARRY TO ME, 21 SEPTEMBER 1927

Well, the banns had been called, the presents were piling up and the scene was set at last. This time Daddy (no doubt resplendent in the outfit that Harry specified) *would* waltz me up the aisle. And I wouldn't be late … .

Chapter 10
Married life—and other adjustments

> I wish you were coming tonight my darlingest. Why,
> it is going to be months and *months before you* dance, I
> don't know—Maladin can be fed on a bottle every
> now and then can't he?
> HARRY TO ME, 18 JANUARY 1929

After our sally down the aisle and the revelries at the Bedford we honeymooned, as planned, in Florence. The weather was kind to us and Harry's aversion to museums and cathedrals, etc. receded as he realised that these places weren't cold the whole year round.

And I finally met his mother, who had recovered pretty well from her illness in January. She definitely had her own style. Grand in a rather soft, perhaps rather Scottish, way, she had immense taste; no wonder she was so comfortable in Italy. Sylvia was a revelation, too: full of confidence and a very personal brand of glamour with the occasional outburst of irritation that Harry had commented on. Take the two of them and I could begin to see where Harry had come from ... .

Having shunted Sylvia off to stay with friends, Alice had rearranged the rooms at the top of her house for us. We were very comfortable and had plenty of privacy.

When we chose to explore and needed a navigator, Sylvia reappeared and proved an excellent guide. Apart from being excellent company and seeming to know everybody, as Harry had noticed, she seemed well versed in the city's cultural and political history. She was also keen on the galleries, not surprisingly, I suppose, when you think of her own artistic skills. In her company we did all the sites. Walked miles in the process.

Harry of course could not resist his former haunts and revelled in showing me off to everybody in Donny's and the other dives that he had frequented ten months earlier. When we decided to be sociable, we partied, danced and (I reckon) dazzled them. I have to say that the Italian men were quite something: handsome, charming, impeccably dressed and, shall we say, very persuasive. We both agreed that this went some way to explaining Sylvia's long interest in the city.

All in all we had a grand time and ventured out into the surrounding hills and the palaces of this or that countess from time to time. And of course Harry knew full well that I would lap up the shops and come away laden with beautiful clothes and shoes: the fabrics, the leathers and the craftsmanship were superb.

Our train tickets allowed us to break our journey anywhere en route and so we made our way back slowly, allowing ourselves time for a stop-off in Paris, where we enjoyed wonderful food and the delights of the Folies Bergère. Then it was back to a new life for us in Lincolnshire: work for Harry and time for us both to set up home. 'Hilltops', the cottage that he had found at Leadenham was going to work well for us. It was about six miles from Cranwell—an easy drive in Daddy's wedding present, a rather whizzy two-seater called a Straker Squire.

Grantham was about eleven miles away to the south and Lincoln some fourteen miles to the north; London was about 120 miles away. I thought we were truly in the sticks.

It was difficult to escape the fact that the surrounding land was flat but fortunately we were on the edge of a rather dramatic rock face the locals called the Trent Cliff; it ran for miles and broke up the skyline rather nicely.

While Harry was at work I had plenty to do with getting

our place straight. We had an embarrassing number of wedding presents to put into service but first I had to find some way of storing them: we could hardly move for all the packages.

As we were both new to the area, we went through the ritual of announcing our arrival and gradually building up a circle of acquaintances, some of whom became friends. This was good news for David—now five—who coped well with the shift from Hove and slowly made playmates. He now had full-time access to Harry, whose stories of his adventures in Mespot and other points East he revelled in. And Harry loved him.

Meanwhile, would you believe, we thought that my dear sister's luck had changed at last. After all the comings and goings (and were they just flirtations or what?) Angela and Bonzo finally began to click. They were together all the time and he finally proposed.

The family was delighted, after all the ups and downs. This wasn't just because of fears that she was getting ever closer to thirty and might never settle; they had always been fond of Bonzo and he did have money which had given him a head start over Harry. Anyway, hallelujah! He proposed and they became engaged. Imagine then, when after eight or nine months of happy planning, she came down to breakfast one morning to find a letter from her fiancé which ran something along the lines of 'by the time you read this I will be on the SS *So-and-So* bound for India; I can't go through with it.' She was devastated and took it very badly. It didn't help that we learned some time later that he went on to meet someone in India and married in 1934. Bonzo really was a naughty boy.

Angela's tragedy ruffled what would otherwise have been a quiet and happy summer. There was plenty of sport at Cranwell for Harry, I began to make some sense of the garden and David soon got the hang of a new tricycle.

I can't really remember if it was David's incessant questions about the whereabouts of 'Harriet' or the bore of rubberwear that prompted our decision to abandon all precaution and take our chances.

Whichever, it didn't take long for us to hit the jackpot and I became pregnant in the spring of 1928. David was excited but, to his dismay, 'Harriet' turned out to be a boy. He wasn't really old enough to realise that this was of course a possibility.

I retreated to stay with Angela in Hove for the birth, expecting this to take place at the local hospital. Not a bit of it. The little mite took the law into his own hands and after frantic calls for a midwife he was born at home on 6 January 1929. Harry was there too, but had to shoot off back to Cranwell after a couple of days, by which time we still hadn't decided what to call 'young Harry'. There was a little tag tied to his toe that read simply 'Baby Reid'—poor little fellow! We were bombarded with suggestions by the whole family and it took a couple of weeks for us to settle on 'Alastair'—a good Scots name, naturally. For some reason this morphed to 'Alasdair' not long afterwards. I can't for the life of me remember why.

While the birth was relatively easy, the wee lad was fairly hard work for the first month or so. What's more, the nurse I had hired turned out to be a disaster: a horrid woman. Fortunately I managed to replace her fairly quickly. As for Harry, while he wallowed in all the congratulations that came our way, he was less understanding about the realities of dealing with an infant. In fact, I'd say he was bloody useless: hadn't a clue about what it all entailed. Being a child himself, you'd think he'd have a better idea than me.

The baby screamed a lot. And then, somehow, the poor mite managed to get a poisoned finger, which made him yell even more. Harry was impossible. There I was, trying to balance the soreness of breastfeeding with endless nights without sleep, and all he could do was voice his impatience about getting back to our nuptial pleasures. It was rather trying. In the end, because his growing interest in getting Wilfred back into action didn't let up, I indulged in a bit of pretence to frighten him off. It seems to have worked:

> Darlingest, wouldn't it be a catastrophe if you find that the close buttock game has lost its charms! They didn't when you had David so let's hope it will be the same now. After all, you say that is the only thing your husband excels himself in, so I am beginning to have doubts about the future because then you won't find your husband at all interesting!
>
> HARRY TO ME, 18 JANUARY 1929

Otherwise things began to settle down. The family was delighted. The boys and I eventually got away from Hove and were back in Leadenham by the beginning of February, by which time, at Harry's insistence, I had taken extensive soundings from Dr Seymour about the 'rubber industry'. My dear husband had a one-track mind, but he wasn't the only person with needs and mine were mainly to avoid another pregnancy—for a while, at least. My aversion made Harry increasingly impatient, which continued to irritate me:

> Haven't any of those rolls of fat and old tummy disappeared yet darling? Of course, they make for comfort but spoil that snaky outline!
>
> HARRY TO ME, 31 JANUARY 1929

Still, he hadn't been completely idle while he was alone. He was even doing his best to be contrite.

> I'm going to try and be human too my darlingest and treat you as nicely as I possibly can—I hate rows and they always depress me for a long time. Let's make up our minds not to have any more my darling. I'm going along to the house this evening to see if the coal and furniture have arrived; also, to

the NAAFI[2] to have the supplies got ready for me to take tomorrow. I am taking rations tomorrow too so there will be plenty to eat in the house.

HARRY TO ME, 4 FEBRUARY 1929

The house was indeed ready for us and, after a month in his rooms at the mess, he was very happy to escape. More to the point he had managed to find us a cook. And equally important, the new nurse was settling in well.

Spring came. My figure returned and I could get into my clothes again. We settled down and Alasdair began to put on weight at last. David soon came to terms with the reality of having a brother and Harry enjoyed them both.

We eased into what became a lovely summer. By now the garden was full of colour, our social life had taken off and David had graduated to two wheels. By now Harry had decided that I no longer posed a risk to other motorists or the public and allowed me to take the two-seater all over the place with David, as my passenger, bubbling with delight.

By September we felt confident enough to leave the nurse and children with the family at Hove and join a gang of friends for a holiday in the Belgian seaside resort at Le Zoute. It was all very jolly and while nothing too improper took place, I seem to remember that we were all rather frisky.

As for the family around this time, my parents carried on at Helouan. As usual, they continued to argue periodically. Daddy would escape to Scotland in search of salmon and Mama would set herself up in some London hotel for a while, catch up on friends and theatre and generally lick her wounds. Angela continued to have 'near misses' and, sadly, was more

---

[2] NAAFI stands for 'Navy, Army and Air Force Institutes', a charity founded in 1920 to provide shopping and recreational facilities for British military personnel and their families.

successful at bridge than men—unfair really, as she was a very good-looking girl. So it often fell to her to accompany Mama on her various escapes, both in England and occasionally on cruises to exotic places further east.

While easy-going brother Nick made progress in the Navy, brainy brother Michael struggled to find the right slot in life. This changed rather dramatically when he met Barbara, the daughter of a marble importer who lived in Brighton and who hired him. In time he became a director of the company but, before that, he was assigned to work in Burma and travelled to Rangoon early in 1929.

It was around this time that, to Harry's delight, Sylvia returned to England. As the family funds had now run dry, she was under maternal notice to earn her own living, so she learned Pitman's shorthand and launched herself into a secretarial career. Her first job, with some ghastly duchess, was a fiasco but after a brief flirtation with the world of beauty culture she landed a plum job at the Iraqi Delegation in London—as secretary to a bigshot in their government called Nuri al-Said. She stayed with him for almost twenty years.

Inevitably the RAF decided that it was time for Harry to move on. To be fair, he'd been at Cranwell far longer than expected and had only really survived because they hadn't managed to find a better qualified person to organise the cadet's gym and PT activities, a function which he had carried out alongside his flying instruction duties. We learned that he was to be an experimental and test pilot at Farnborough, so we packed up and made our way there in mid-July 1929. I must say, they gave us a grand send-off. Farewell to the Fens.

How best to describe Farnborough? Not the most exciting place on Earth: really rather ghastly, surrounded by the military —Aldershot, Frimley, Camberley; one couldn't escape. But the Surrey Hills and lovely walks were not very far away, and that made a welcome change from the 'flat' of Lincolnshire. We lived at a place called Pinehurst Grange, just at the north-east corner of the airfield. Our house was called 'Monksway'. What a hoot! I have heard Harry called any number of things but nobody would ever have described him as in any way 'monkish'.

The place where Harry worked was properly called the Royal Aircraft Establishment. His work was rather hush-hush and as far as I could understand his main job was to take up boffins so that they could test equipment of one kind or another. More like a glorified taxi driver if you ask me.[3]

In August we returned to La Zoute with a rather quieter group than the year before—just as well, as we took the children this time. They loved the sea. And Harry—resplendent in a really garish striped swimming costume—proved a dab hand at building sandcastles.

One way and another we made our house into a real home. I got the garden into good shape and we had some lovely luncheon parties. David was doing well at school. And we bought a toy car for Alasdair.

We were there the best part of three years. Harry missed the rural sports which had kept him happy in the early Cranwell days, particularly the shooting, but he did get in some decent cricket and we both improved our tennis.

There was even the occasional flash of glitz, in particular in 1931 when we went to what was called the 'Fourth Court of the Season' at Buckingham Palace. This really was *the* moment to dig out the glad rags—and we did not disappoint. I

---

[3] Harry worked with several specialist teams, beginning with the Instrument and Photographic Flight, which assessed everything from oxygen equipment and landing gear to cameras and smoke screen testing. Later, he worked on just about every aspect of wireless communication and then on engine research. This included his first flight in a Westland Wapiti which he would later fly operationally in India. He also had a go at testing Schneider Trophy racing aircraft.

Us in The Mall, about to attend Court at Buckingham Palace, 1931.

borrowed Mama's tiara, to top a super silk gown complete with sweeping train. Harry was togged up in full dress. We waited for ages in the Mall for our 'carriage' to be called and then I curtsied to the Queen at a grand ceremony inside the palace.

High Society indeed! We even got our picture in the paper.

And then everything turned upside down. Little David died suddenly at the end of November. He was staying with Mama at Helouan. One minute he was alive and apparently well—the next minute he had gone. How on Earth could this happen? Why hadn't someone spotted the warning signs that must have been there? Was I somehow to blame?

I couldn't bear the thought of his being cut up but I knew there would have to be an autopsy. It revealed an abscess in his gut. It had burst, poisoning his blood and killing him horribly quickly. He was nine; such a bright, happy child. A light snuffed out—just like that. We buried him in a corner for young people at the church at Hove where Harry and I married.

It crippled us all. Having tried to care for him over the years, Daddy thought that he and Dr Seymour had in some way failed. Mama in turn felt guilty because it was she who had wanted him to visit. And neither Harry nor I was there when David died. Bless my mother, she promised to look after David's grave after we went back to Farnborough—and she did, keeping it up for over ten years.

Little Alasdair was not yet three when David disappeared from our lives. He couldn't understand where he had gone. The thing that hurt most was that suddenly, no one wanted to talk about him. That was how people behaved in those days. It took all of us years to get over it; in the process, we quietened down quite a lot. We were less exuberant. We still made the occasional trip up to London but preferred to retreat to Brighton when we wanted a change. While we both mourned the loss of a delightful little boy, I struggled with the added burden of seeing my own child buried and what felt like the final severance of my life with Horace. Harry was considerate about this: he understood completely.

My parents were traumatised by the whole experience. While we did our best to lick our wounds, Mama decided that she had to get away from Helouan and its memories, and a new

Margaret, Daddy, Alasdair in front, and Angela at Highdown, July.

house hunt ensued. The two of them finally settled on a house at 40 Dyke Road Avenue called Highdown. Dyke Road Avenue provided the main entry to Brighton from the north and Highdown was one of a small number of earlier houses at the northern end. It was a fairly substantial pile, set back from the road, with plenty of garden at front and back and surrounded by walls to ensure privacy; I suppose you might describe it as 'mock-Tudor'. Mama liked its presence but thought it miles from anywhere. Daddy however, wanted to swap the gentility of central Hove for the peace of the Downs, less than a mile away.

Years later the move proved to have been a mixed blessing. Mama despaired at the cost of running the place and spent ages trying to persuade Daddy to move, but it did save them from the bombs that tore up Brighton in the war.

Around this time there was an incident to which I still look back with shame. After Angela had been dumped by Bonzo, she became bizarrely curious about Harry's performance in bed and allowed her fascination to grew into an outrageous and monotonous obsession, to the extent that she would try it discuss it with me when we were together, and found it hard to look away from Harry if he was around. One day, in exasperation, I foolishly suggested that if she was so bloody curious, why didn't she try him out? Harry, whom I told about this afterwards, wasn't sure what to make of it but Angela took me at my word, got hold of him one day when they were both in the back of a taxi and decided to find out for herself—in broad daylight! You may wonder what the driver was up to during this wild and sordid event, and whether the taxi was on the move or parked somewhere. I don't know. But then Brighton is Brighton.

When I heard about it after, I think I was more annoyed with myself than with Harry. There wasn't a post mortem as such, but Angela did reveal that Harry's gifts knocked Bonzo out of the ring. Without any question, one way or another, Harry—the rotten so-and-so—was a willing accomplice. He couldn't deny it. He didn't deny it. He even enjoyed it. I was furious. It's the only time in our marriage when I really wanted to hit him. Somehow, though, I managed to take enough deep breaths to stop myself. Close thing, you might say. And fortunately, we left for India not long afterwards, and that gave us all the chance to cool off. Looking back, I recognise that having failed to snag a man, Angela was hungry and deeply envious of what I took for granted. But there were also times when I wondered if the whole thing wasn't a wee piece of Angela's revenge on me for pinching all her boyfriends when we were younger ... .

In the end, the story got out and eventually the whole family knew. It was beyond embarrassing—but it was also complicated by other elements to the story that I haven't come to yet.

In a way it was a relief when we returned to East Anglia the following May. Farnborough had become claustrophobic and the change—this time to Martlesham in Suffolk—was welcome. The RAF assessed Harry's flying as 'exceptional' just before we left. It cheered him up.

This time his job was to put the various inventions developed at Farnborough to the test in normal service flight. He also flew new prototype aircraft, several of which, such as the Hawker Hart and Wapiti, came into RAF service. As far as Harry was concerned this counted as 'fun': flinging these planes around the sky and seeing what they could do was just up his street.

At some point the RAF sent him on a course at Old Sarum —something to do with 'cooperation with army operations'. We didn't know it at the time, but this was what he would do for the next three years or so. It didn't take long for us to find out however: early in 1933 we packed our bags once again and this time boarded the SS *California* to sail to Bombay.

Little sahibs: Alasdair and friends, rather wedged between two humps.

Chapter 11
Frontier days

> The Mahsud or Wazir is an expert at attacking convoys or small detachments and is assisted by the nature of his country, the ravines being narrow and winding, while the hillsides … are often thickly covered in bushes. He attacks systematically, with special parties being told off for specific duties, such as the neutralisation of adjacent picquets by fire, support to his advanced parties of swordsmen etc. Ambushes may sometimes open by a few shots from one side of a nullah. Untrained troops rush to cover on the side from which the fire comes. This is what is waited for. Heavy accurate fire from the other bank then finishes the party.
>
> PAMPHLET ISSUED BY HQ WAZIRISTAN DISTRICT, 1924

[At this point, your humble author has to intervene once again to provide a little more context and to fill in a few factual gaps that Margaret was not au fait with.

The region on India's north-western border with Afghanistan was known as the North-West Frontier and was to be Margaret's home for the next three years. It was far from peaceful. The British administration had found itself in conflict in this region repeatedly since the 1830s when the 'Great Game' with the Russian Empire began, a seventy-seven-year period of strategic rivalry between the British Empire and the Russian Empire for dominance in Central Asia, driven by mutual suspicion and competing imperial ambitions.

The area is isolated, mountainous and difficult to control. The British (as represented by the East India Company which governed India until 1858) feared that the Russian Army would come through the North-West Frontier to invade India—either themselves, by force, or by persuading Afghan and local North-West frontiersmen to rise up against British control. In consequence, the British military strove to exercise control over Afghanistan by stationing large numbers of troops in the buffer zone between the two countries and stamping its authority on the local Pashtun tribes.

Attempts to secure British interests in Afghanistan by diplomatic means were studded by intrigue, betrayal and military interventions, none of which could be claimed as having been successful. Beginning with the First Anglo-Afghan War from 1838 to 1842, there followed a second (1878 to 1880) and a third in 1919—all in some way connected with the so-called 'Great Game' with Russia.

In parallel, the British faced a long series of actions against local tribesmen opposed to British rule, involving an almost endless series of punitive expeditions that began in the 1880s and continued throughout the 1930s. In local tribesmen they faced a formidable foe.

But by then, the Army and the Air Force had started to coordinate their movements. While the RAF had a policing role on the North-West Frontier, Harry's training in aerial cooperation with Army activities would help the RAF to reach remote villages easily, subdue unrest, gather reconnaissance, bomb and intimidate, all more quickly and less expensively than if the same operations were carried out by ground forces.

Margaret was about to enter another war zone … .]

Me—in Quetta!

In February 1933 we returned to the heat and dust, this time to a place called Quetta, in what is now Baluchistan, one of the four provinces of modern-day Pakistan. We were just inside India and near Afghanistan's southern border. The British had apparently been there for over fifty years. Kandahar—over the border—was just 140 miles away.

We were high up—somewhere around 5,500 ft—and while the mercury easily reached 100°F in the summer, you could easily get twenty inches of snow over the winter. Fortunately, the monsoon rains didn't reach Quetta but we did experience one pretty formidable twister: it really shook the place up. We had a pretty little bungalow with a charming garden, not far from the airfield in the ridiculously English-sounding Lytton Road, and soon added a dog of very questionable origins that we called 'Peter'. Alasdair, just four and happy as a sandboy, loved the dog. Boy and dog must have developed a cast-iron gut because they were hardly ever sick and our servants kept both of them happily amused. I spent my days reading, playing bridge and gardening—to the extent that the *mali* would let me, for flowers were *his* territory. He did allow me to dabble with shrubs and vegetables, however.

Quetta itself was a bundle of grub and fascination, which we enjoyed exploring. Alasdair was fascinated by the bazaars and particularly fond of the camels.

As for entertainment, there was a gymkhana club complete with swimming pool where we would gather, often moving on to a lunch party somewhere. We would often escape for picnics in a beautiful valley to the east of the city where there was a huge reservoir called Hanna Lake. Surrounded by mountains, it was a lovely place to relax.

Further away there were places like Ziarat, a town about eighty miles to the east, where it was much cooler. The only

A delightful lunch party at Quetta, with me and Harry on the right.

trouble was that the road was unbelievably rocky, which meant that we really did bounce our way there and back.

Somehow it felt different to Mespot. For a start, the British had been in India for far longer and their influence was much stronger. In general I think that we were somehow closer to the Indians than the Arabs or Kurds, and I like to think that we treated each other well. Other people have told me the same.

Harry always regarded the tribesmen with great respect and, when required to fight them later on, would nevertheless respect them as formidable warriors.

Harry was with No. 5 Squadron. He flew planes called Wapitis—two-seater bi-planes that he had tested in his Martlesham days and which were specially designed to cope with the heat and dust of colonial ops (*see below*). We knew of course that the North-West Frontier, where we had been scrapping with the locals since God knows when, was broadly unstable and it fell to the Army and Air Force to deal with outbreaks that threatened the Empire as and when they occurred.

As far as I could see, Harry spent that first year there training his flight to support the army: reconnoitring this place, photographing that place, dropping supplies here and there, and practising attacks.

All the while lots was going on at home. For a start, both Nick and Michael were married: Nick to a rather lovely girl called Bunty in a classic naval 'do' at Plymouth and Michael (at last) to Barbara, whom we thought was rather less spirited but nevertheless very well connected in Brighton. Mike himself was struggling to adjust after more than three years in Rangoon. That just left Angela; would she ever find someone? Daddy and Mama, however, were still scrapping: his letters were full of agitation about money or politics while hers were generally full of doom and gloom.

A Westland Wapiti of No. 5 Squadron. Harry flew it brilliantly.

At the end of the year Harry took his flight down to a place near Poona for joint exercises with the Army—way south of Bombay. He was away for the best part of a month and, apart from a brief period when Alasdair was born, this was the first time we had been separated in six years of married life. We wrote to each other almost daily, and traded increasing dollops of saucy chitchat. I sent him some rather naughty sketches but couldn't persuade him to take photos of Wilfred, probably because he couldn't trust the people who developed the film.

> Wilfred is wondering why the hell he hasn't had any exercise just lately. He is beginning to miss it very much, he is very big and handsome and liable to peep out beneath my shorts at any moment, which reminds me I must see that he keeps in his place at this cocktail party this morning. Perhaps I'd better put a big ribbon on him just in case he did look out.
>
> HARRY TO ME, 3 DECEMBER 1933

Harry stopped at some fairly exotic places and palaces on the way, and was treated like royalty. He particularly liked an old fort that towered over a hilltop outside Jodhpur. As for the city itself, Alasdair pricked up his ears when I reported that his daddy had seen a Morris Minor that the Maharajah had ordered for his son, and which had a top speed of fifteen miles an hour. Alasdair wanted one ... .

> My darlingest Margaret. Here we are at Jodhpur after a very good trip. I wish you could be here with me; it is a marvellous place after Quetta and this hotel is really very fine too. Poor master missed having his darling little wife in bed last night. Isn't it sad that we won't be together again for another month. At Hyderabad we did nothing but fill up the aeroplanes and have a quick lunch—which was very good— we then took off and got here at 5:30 ... You will be glad

to hear that we are all state guests, everything is free and we have a couple of cars at our disposal to do what we like with.

HARRY TO ME, 24 NOVEMBER 1933

Of course, Harry could never keep his vanity at bay:

> You'll be jealous to hear that a woman at Ahmedabad said, 'who is that man, my God he's the best-looking man I've seen.' We were at the club at the time playing billiards so of course I had to have a dance with her! I had two dances altogether, one with this wench and one with a beaky nosed flagpole.
>
> HARRY TO ME, 27 NOVEMBER 1933

He got his comeuppance when he reached his final destination—a camp somewhere in the middle of nowhere where life was far from cushy and Wilfred became increasingly lonely. He really didn't like the idea of me getting too fond of the Christmas party scene and possible 'hostile' advances from the young lads at the mess.

> You will be getting too strong a liking for Champagne my darling after all these parties. I hope it won't mean that you would rather I stayed away because there doesn't seem to be so much flowing when I am there!
>
> HARRY TO ME, 12 DECEMBER 1933

After what sounded like a fairly riotous send-off from the army at Poona, Harry made it back to Quetta on Christmas Eve and peace was happily restored. But he had missed out on a wonderfully festive month. The Quetta children had even had a visit from Santa (by plane).

In spite of the snow we relaxed with picnics and managed a little exploring—the mountains were spectacular. And Oh, I was glad to have brought my furs. Harry got some shooting in, bagged some game and later I joined him on some of his fishing trips. The spring brought flowers and hockey.

And then I began to get slightly mysterious letters from Angela, coupled with further elaboration from Mama. A chap called Maurice Whittome, a barrister, was keen on her and was writing to her with ever-increasing frequency. She was definitely weakening. The pair had been acquainted for some time—Maurice had been at our wedding—and his family lived at Steyning, a village not far away near Haywards Heath. His father owned a large chunk of Brighton, so the cash registers may have been tinkling.

Well, I wished her luck and kept my fingers firmly crossed.

All in all, life was not bad. Harry's work was not very onerous and as far as I could gather the squadron spent most of its time mucking about alongside the army in readiness for the local disturbances that erupted from time to time. So plenty of practice flying: bombing, photography, dummy forced landings and close ground support (which I think meant flying suicidally close to terra firma), etc. After Kurdistan, Harry had a pretty good idea about flying in mountainous territory and did his best to pass this on to the youngsters in his flight. They of course were in awe of him: that medal ribbon with sloping purple and white stripes—his DFC—carried huge kudos. There was plenty of time too for cricket and tennis, at least until the rains arrived.

Near the end of the year we moved to Peshawar—right into frontier territory, where Waziri tribesmen had been doing their best to disrupt the British for years. There were rumbles that trouble might be on the way ...

Afghanistan was only thirty miles distant and the border was pretty porous, as far as the tribesmen were concerned: they came and went as they pleased. Peshawar was an ancient city, full of character and even hotter than Quetta. It also had a thriving set of small workshops making guns of all kinds: they could copy anything from an army rifle to an automatic pistol. The locals were all armed to the teeth—quite scary—and talking of the locals, the men were incredibly handsome, resplendent in magnificent beards and moustaches.

Harry was now with No. 20 Squadron—still working with the army and flying Wapitis. He liked them: they seemed to take any amount of punishment (of which there was plenty).

Somehow service life was better set up at Peshawar. We lived in a nice bungalow in the RAF compound that came with a very comfortable veranda that was perfect for entertaining. We had plenty of friends and there were 'amusements' of many kinds including the pantomimes and other amateur dramatic efforts in which we were happy to clown to our hearts' content.

Hanna Monsters' party: Harry on the left, me on the right. July 1934.

This time the *mali* was far less possessive and I kept myself busy with the garden. What with keeping up with friends, looking after Alasdair and reading more and more books I had heaps to do. There was plenty of sport too—cricket and shooting for Harry and tennis for me. We were happy.

Alasdair thrived. He became a cub and in his own way very much a young *sahib*. Add to this his passable performance at school, great enthusiasm for his Scots blood and kilt and a growing obsession with cars, and he was doing well. Whether passable was good enough, as far as his education was concerned, we were unsure and we began to think about what to do to improve matters, but for the time being he was a happy member of the family and we all loved him. We laughed a lot.

Alasdair with his garage at Peshawar: his love of cars started early.

Alasdair with me at Pindi, April 1936. 'Great enthusiasm for his kilt.'

Bombs in readiness at Peshawar, 1935. Things were getting 'hot'.

Early in 1935 there were the first signs that things might get 'hot'. Parties of tribesmen began to stir up trouble in the Swat valley, northwest of Peshawar, which later spread to the east. The disturbance escalated and Harry flew on various sorties, starting with bomb and machine gun attacks on those who were proving dangerous.

There were more bombing strikes a couple of months later and then quiet. I'm not sure if one ever gets used to being shot at but while Harry had plenty of experience of this, I was always relieved to see him come home safely.

We had just got over this business when, on 31 May, Quetta suffered a terrible earthquake, one of the most severe to have hit that part of the world. And that's where we had been only six months previously. Harry's No. 5 Squadron colleagues were still there and were badly clobbered when the camp got completely destroyed. The airman's quarters were flattened along with several of the officers' bungalows, including the one that used to be ours. Those who did get out had a terrible time trying to rescue their friends while struggling with fresh tremors, falling debris and other horrors. Surrounding towns and villages were obliterated and thousands were buried in the rubble. Heaven knows how many people died.

Somehow the hangars stayed upright but only three of the twenty-seven aircraft inside them remained fit to fly. The army used light tanks to pull the roofs off the buildings so that they could rescue those buried beneath. As for the Indians themselves, we heard any number of tales about their resilience and resourcefulness.

Several of Harry's fellow pilots flew medicines and other stuff from Peshawar as part of the relief operation; he was unhappy not to have joined them. When he did get there a couple of months later he was relieved to find many of our old friends still alive.[1] The town was devastated. The camp was now under canvas.[2]

In July Alasdair and I headed for the hills to cool down. We were at a place called Nathia Gali in the Murree Hills, which was a small village with a rather nice little church some 140 miles east of Peshawar. The Resident's house was the largest building there and hosted plenty of parties and tennis. Harry kept me supplied with fruit and a steady stream of books from the camp library while he did his best not to get too bored in the heat. He also did his best to liaise between me and the *dhazi* — the tailor—who was doing a sterling job of making dresses for me and shirts for him, and of speaking English. The *dhazi*'s fluency in English dress-making terms far outstripped Harry's.

Still, Harry wrote nice long letters full of not very much, except when bellyaching about the slow progress on renovating our bungalow; but there was the occasional nice thought:

---

[1] Altogether the RAF lost one officer, fifty-three British Other Ranks and two children, of whom the officer, eighteen British and seventeen Indian Other Ranks were from 5 Squadron.
[2] As for No. 5 Squadron, the unit eventually moved to Chaklala near Rawalpindi in October 1935.

> I'm glad you have decided to wear black evening dresses this winter, you look damn fine in black.
>
> HARRY TO ME, 10 SEPTEMBER 1935

By the time I returned to Peshawar in September 1935 they had shifted Harry from flying to squadron admin. While he was a bit nonplussed about this, it filled me with some relief, as the squadron was busy supporting soldiers struggling with large numbers of tribesmen in the valleys and being shot at from the hills and I wanted him out of this.

This operation, known as the Second Mohmand Campaign, went on until November. Yes, I was more than happy that Harry was on the ground for most of the time.

Meanwhile I missed all the fun back in Brighton. Angela had at last married Maurice. It was a joyful time and I should have been there. Harry had missed out too: his brother Toby had married a girl called Bunny whom he had met in Malaya.

Over the next year Harry gradually did less and less flying. The Wapitis had gone, replaced by a newer model called the Audax, and Harry got promoted to squadron leader and returned to No. 5 Squadron as CO. He was very happy about this, not surprisingly, and of course with the salary increase that came with it. In turn, this entailed another move and we shifted to Rawalpindi.

By this time I needed a break. So, to Harry's dismay and my insistence, I took Alasdair back to England early in the spring, leaving Harry in grass-widow mode for a few months. At last I could check on my newly married siblings: and they were fine.

Harry did manage to get to England for a while in July and we enjoyed much of the summer together, catching up with family and friends, among other things. We also managed to fit in a trip up to Newtyle, where Harry was born, and meet his Aunt Bessie, a formidable woman who also had a heart of gold. She doted on Alasdair—made him feel a proper Scot.

While we were together, Harry and I gave much thought to

Alasdair's schooling. We agreed that arrangements in Pindi were rather limited. What to do? Harry's know-all colleagues had all said the same: 'Send him to boarding school in England—that's what we do.' Poor lad. He was only seven and the thought of my returning to India without him terrified me; wasn't losing one child enough? In the end, hoping that my parents would agree to help, we decided we should find a school not too far from Brighton and leave him there when I went back. And that's what I did; Mama and Daddy agreed that education had to come before anything else, and so the die was cast.

Together, we enrolled Alasdair at a prep school in Eastbourne called St Andrews, but it was I who dropped him off and left him there, because Harry had returned to India ahead of me. So, for ages, it was *me* whom he blamed for everything in the letters he was forced to write every Sunday. When he felt like it, he would let me have it with both barrels:

Horrid schweinhund. You ought to be ashamed of yourself because you haven't written to me for 2, 2½ or 3 weeks you disgraceful young pig, you are a thoughtless old woman. ... I wish you were drowned on your ship.

ALASDAIR TO MARGARET, 15 FEBRUARY 1937

It really hurt.

Harry had returned to India just in time to marshal his team for the All-India Inter-Command shooting competition, which they duly won. That boring old picture of the winning team is still on the wall downstairs.

As I have already said, Harry was a fully paid-up member of the huntin', shootin' and fishin' club and was a crack shot—he won medals all over the place. He had a beautiful pistol—a Remington automatic. He once stalked a crow with the thing, fired and killed it at a range of seventy yards.

He could however be very careless. While he would always go on about safety with guns, a few months later he was in a

Harry (seated, centre) and the victorious shooting team, 1936.

concrete pillbox, safe from enemy fire, and managed to drop his revolver on the ground. It went off; the bullet ricocheted all over the place but missed all the occupants. I still squirm at the thought.

Two or three months after I got back to Pindi, Harry and several planes moved to a place called Miranshah, some 200 miles away to the southwest.

From what I gleaned from the other wives, there was an army op against Wazirs in the Khaisora valley and the RAF was instructed to help them out. Harry flew one or two recce sorties but then he stayed on the ground while his men dealt with the dangerous stuff: offensives against tribesmen attacking our troops, and strikes on their bases.

He came back for a while on Christmas Eve only to return a couple of weeks later. He did one more attack sortie and flew the top dog on his first inspection flight of Waziristan District in late March. You know, he had great respect for the NWF tribesmen: they reminded him of the Kurds. A day later he flew for the last time in India. What we did not realise at the time was that this flight would effectively mark the end of his operational service career, as he spent the rest of his time with the RAF flying a desk. But more of that later. For now, he had finished his tour in India and was due for home leave.

Harry in unorthodox kit at Miranshah, 1936.

By then I too had had enough of being a grass widow. On top of this, Mama moved on from her endless tirades about Edward VIII, which thankfully ceased when he abdicated in December, to alarming us with reports that Alasdair had been ill (but was now recovered). It was time for us both to go home.

They played us out in style, with parties at various clubs ending up with a final picnic trip up to Landi Kotal half way up the Khyber Pass.

On our way to Lahore we stopped off at Chillianwala to visit the memorial to those killed in the Second Sikh War; Harry's idea of course but I was really quite moved—and his grandfather, Major General James Reid, had fought there. Once at Delhi we did the city and all its glory—forts, gates, churches, mosques and tombs—the lot, including as many relics of the mutiny as Harry could find. We then went on to Agra and ticked the Taj Mahal off our list—unspoilt, quiet and surrounded by trees and flowers—so beautiful.

I remember that it was at that point that I put my foot down and vetoed a diversion to Lucknow, where Harry's grandfather had also fought during the 1858 mutiny.

Instead, we motored on to Bombay and boarded the SS *City of London*, reaching London on 8 May 1937 after a comfortable month at sea. We were just in time for the Coronation of King George. As a Lieutenant of the City of London, Papa was one of the great and the good who attended the service.

We had a wonderful summer. Alasdair gradually forgave us and we found aged relatives, plus Angela, Nick, Mike and their spouses, in the pink. We slipped in a few days of seaside at Wittering at the end of June, before hiving off to the Bavarian Alps, meeting friends at Lake Constance and then drifting up the Rhine towards Heidelberg. All quite delightful. Then in August it was time for Harry to report back for work, so off we went to a base just south of Odiham, a pretty, little village sandwiched between Farnborough and Basingstoke, and with more history than both of them put together.

To crown the summer off, we went up to Bond Street at some point to see a series of ballet paintings that Sylvia was exhibiting. My, my, the girl had talent; Harry was very proud of his little sister.

After that, it was back to school for Alasdair. He was growing up fast and looked very smart in his uniform— Eton collars, the lot. How he had struggled at first with the studs that attached the collar to his shirt!

And then of course there was the whole business of getting used to being back in England. We missed the gentle knocks on the door announcing the arrival of bed tea; fresh chapatis; the mountains. And as for those beautiful men ...

But there were plenty of compensations. For one thing, we didn't miss the dust. And there were new dances to learn and wardrobes to replenish ... .

Below is illustrated a good looking single-breasted suit in a Glen check saxony cloth. He is correctly dressed for the country race meeting; his accessories include chamois gloves, dark brown soft felt hat and umbrella.

Back in England, Harry cuts a dash.

South and Central America: the black dots represent towns on the Pacific coast that Harry and I visited, 1938–42.

Chapter 12
To Chile

> Today Steve and I went to an attachés' lunch at the country club and then came back here instead of going to the Legation as it was about 4 when we got back. Everybody here has been asking about you and sending loves so you should be flattered! The *'veinte ocho'* [Peruvian Independence Day] is going to be a strenuous day—Forbes calls here for us at 8.30 then we go to the Te Deum, then palace, then a parade at the old racecourse so we probably won't get back until fairly late probably feeling very weary as we may have to stand for a long time.
> HARRY TO ME, 26 JULY 1939

Our relaxation in England was short-lived. In July '38 we travelled to Chile where Harry began life as an assistant air attaché. As we had been told to expect a lot of travel in the region and we didn't want to muck up Alasdair's schooling any more, we left him behind at St Andrew's with Daddy and Mama once again *in loco parentis*. Do you know, I think that was when it all began to go wrong? We didn't realise it then; in those days there was nothing odd about packing children off to board at the age of eight (well, almost eight …). And it did give us lots of time to ourselves. And how were we to know that we would be away for four years—not only that, but a war would begin a year later that would really complicate our lives.

It started off so easily. Lazy, delicious, slow boat to Buenos Aires. Stop off at Madeira with enough time for tea with

Sporting my RAF brooch for my flight over the Andes.

friends at Reid's Hotel and then a day at St Vincent before the last leg to Argentina. Déjà vu for Harry, who seemed lost in thoughts of his childhood. And who should meet us but my cousin Pat, a stalwart in the strong British community that

Diplomats process on Peruvian Independence Day. Harry is circled.

thrived in BA. It was exciting. Harry reported to the British Mission to which he was attached and learned that he was to be based at Lima, looking after all the countries on the Pacific coast from Chile to Colombia—stretching well over 5,000 miles. His job was to keep close to the national air forces in the area, arrange visits and exchanges and generally represent HMG in military matters. He also had to report on the state of their airfields, aircraft and their readiness and such. Quite how much this involved 'spying' I never really knew, but he certainly got around, flitting from legation to legation—often flying himself. He certainly knew a lot about the airfields in the region.

Why did he get the job? Well, he did remember some Spanish from his Argentine childhood. And as someone so distinctly pukka he was admirably qualified, taking to the diplomatic merry-go-round like a duck to water.

And so—on to Peru. Easier said than done, however. We began with a long drive west to Mendoza. I remember grumbling about the road and later thinking that this was plain sailing compared with many that we drove over the following four years. From Mendoza there was but a quick hop over the Andes (17,500 ft) before descending to Santiago and the end of my first encounter with an aeroplane (not so scary after all). After a day's rest we flew north to Arica, the Chilean city just inside the border with Peru, moving on the next day to Lima—over 2,000 miles all told.

Although we had arrived in the middle of winter, it was not unduly cold and we had brought all the right clothes.

While Harry settled in to his office at the British Legation, I wallowed in welcomes from the wives of his various colleagues, who took me to see the sites in and around Lima. And it began to get slightly warmer so I could begin to think about getting out of tweeds. But really, the start didn't go too smoothly. I had been painfully unwell for several months with what turned out to be what they called a 'uterine' fibroid. Everything came to a 'head' in August, as you might say—I was in agony and hadn't even lasted a month. They rushed me to a hospital in Lima and removed my right ovary (*see photo overleaf*). I couldn't care how good or clean the place was. I just wanted it—whatever it was

In my bath chair with my Peruvian nurses on my first day out of bed, 1938.

—sorted out. It scared Harry out of his wits. My dear doctor daddy might have been a little more sympathetic, commenting that the growth was 'only the size of a walnut'. On top of that he reckoned I should still be able to 'give Alistair a sister' (and get a move on—cheeky blighter!)

I recovered quickly under the 'supervision' of Mrs Forbes, the wife of the Head of the British Mission. She was shall we say formidable both in her manner and her size. Her daughter, much more svelte, offered much more in the way of concrete assistance and was quite delightful. My convalescence began in the lush gardens of the Legation accompanied by beautiful parrots and tea on the lawn. Later I was treated to delightful trips to Chosica, Ancon, Mollendo and other local spots and I began to learn something of the Incas.

Harry meanwhile began to learn the diplomatic ropes, starting with a grand diplomatic procession and parade to celebrate Peruvian Independence Day at Lima on 28 July. I must say he scrubbed up most handsomely in his full ceremonial fig. When I think about it, his job was rather hard to define. He was there to support our ambassador and was certainly meant to get pally with the local air force wherever he was while keeping a close eye on their airfields and what have you. And of course, he represented the RAF at all manner of national and local events. Yes, there must have been a certain element of spying in all this and that must have been one of the reasons why he travelled to all those countries. (I think they called it 'gathering intelligence'.)

In September we finally reached Santiago where we set ourselves up at Bilbao 2296. We lived there until my return home the next year. Over the next few months we really had a good time—somehow people were set on as much fun as they could muster and we were only too happy to join in.

I remember excellent fishing at Pucon in December, seeing in 1939 at a jolly party at Vina del Mar, seaside frolics at Concon in January and a wonderful fishing trip at John

Peruvian women with their llama—the Peruvian 'beast of burden'.

Chadwick's shack up in the hills at Panguipulli—all within spitting distance of Santiago. Later on we went 1,850 miles south to the Straights of Magellan and saw penguins and silver foxes with the marvels of the Patagonian Andes looming above us.

Closer to Easter, we went up Chilean canals for a long watery holiday with friends in a ferry called the SS *Muraled* that took us around the Chilean Lake District. This time we were about 750 miles south of Santiago—just south of Pucon. We crammed in wonderful scenery, excellent fishing and a lot of alcohol. Perhaps the most stunning site was the Osorno volcano to the east of a beautiful lake called Llanquihue (at least, I think that is what it is called). It was shaped like a perfect cone and towered up to almost 9,000 ft. Breathtaking. Somehow Harry managed to squeeze in some time for work.

As for me, I was entranced by such colourful people, their animals, the boats and the mountains. Yet again I was struck by the strength of the women, their clothes and the textiles that made them. We were seeing life as few others would—and all in the name of Harry's 'work'.

And Santiago itself was a jolly place to be. We had a lovely house complete with delightful servants and a swimming pool —and of course the mongrel puppy that Harry scooped up

Harry with his catch from the Rio Petrohue (the Chilean Lake District).

somewhere along the way. The buzz and glamour of the diplomatic merry-go-round swept us up, although Harry moaned about tediously long parades. Travel, parties, receptions, tennis, Latin exotica and romance ... life in Santiago was easy. The climate wasn't too bad, even though eighty degrees at Christmas time didn't seem quite right. We found time for tennis and bridge, flirted a lot, entertained and danced endlessly and managed to navigate the social scene pretty well—the Prince of Wales club in particular was a popular haunt. Gossip of course was rife—who was who, the occasional scandal, idle speculation here and there and grumbles about servants were grist to the mill. We also drank and smoked too much—no wonder my lungs are all shot now ...

Travel was tricky; rattletrap lorries with doped-up drivers; narrow, rough roads on mountain sides and local airplanes to be avoided at all costs. Harry had a nasty reminder about overzealous drivers when he had a narrow escape in February after his taxi overturned on a very rough road.

And we got around a lot. It was part of the job—after all, what better excuse for being somewhere than being on holiday?

Apart from muddles due to the very unpredictable postal service, everything seemed to be under control in England. Alasdair's writing became even harder to read. When not complaining about a lack of letters from us (not always fair) most of his letters were about our choice of car (and why we shouldn't have bought it); we never managed to persuade him that Chile wasn't stuffed full of English cars ...

By mid-'39 we had been living it up in South America for over a year. All the same I was homesick and, prodded by parents who clearly thought we had neglected Alasdair and my own worries about Angela and a nightmare second pregnancy, I decided to make a short trip home for the summer.

In the run-up to this I joined Harry in June for the first of his official 'inspection' tours. I never quite worked out just what he 'inspected' but he did visit any number of mines (nitrates, phosphates … even gold) as well as all the airfields he could find up and down the west coast. Our *expedición grande* took us all the way up the Pacific coast to Bolivia and began when we boarded the Grace Line liner *Santa Clara* at Valparaiso and made our way up to Callao, the port at Lima, before sailing on to Guayaquil in Ecuador for the first leg of the trip.

From there we made our way over the 250 or so miles to Quito on a weird railway that took forever as we veered from coast through jungle, mountainsides of forest and finally reached the foot of the Andes. (Have you ever been on a train that looks more like a motor car?)

Eventually we climbed to over 9,000 ft and found this extraordinary old, crumbling city. The air was very thin, but in spite of being winter it was dry and not too cold. Apart from the formalities of Harry's visit, we found clubs, beautiful gardens and women wearing funny hats everywhere—half-way between a bowler and a trilby. What on earth they thought of the sight of us resplendent in our tweeds remains a mystery …

Having made our way back to Guayaquil we moved west to

A halt on the weird railway from Guayaquil to Quito. It's not the GWR.

Quito in 1939, the year in which it hosted the South American Games.

a pretty town called Salinas, which was right on the coast. We found squadrons of pelicans there, huge birds with wingspans of six or seven feet. Come to think of it, Ecuador was full of magnificent birds: we saw condors, eagles, macaws, humming birds and any number of creatures with long tails.

At some point we flew on to Colombia and the capital, Bogota, where—once again—we were treated like royalty.

And then it was time to go home. I left Harry in Cali near the Colombian coast and took a train up to the port at Buenaventura where I boarded the *Santa Clara*, which took me up through the Panama Canal into the Caribbean. I was on my way. I could begin to relax.

The *Santa Clara* was pretty well set up: day times spent reading, swimming, atrocious attempts at deck quoits and occasional flirtation with the senior crew, who were all decked up in white. Dinner was formal and the dance band had occasional good moments. We were all excited to go through the canal: all those huge locks—it took well over ten hours to do the 40 miles or so that separate the two oceans. Once in the Caribbean we sailed up to Havana, where we landed for a few hours before steaming up the East Coast of the USA and then we crowded on deck to spot the Statue of Liberty, the Manhattan skyline and New York itself. Years later I heard that the *Santa Clara* was sunk during the 1944 Normandy landings.

After a few delightful (and expensive) days in New York with friends I boarded the *Aquitania* for the voyage back to England. After *Santa Clara*, *Aquitania* was huge—a beautiful ship. They said she was 26 years old—pretty old for a Cunard-White Star Line vessel but welcoming just the same. She landed me safely at Southampton in August and I headed for home.

Back in Hove, I had a couple of delightful weeks to catch up with Alasdair before he went back to school. He was ten by now and how he had grown. And—to his joy—was resplendent now in long trousers. As well as cars, he was now obsessed with his bicycle—speeding around as fast as he could and dreaming of ways to go faster.

I revelled in the reunion with the family and friends and was very happy to find Angela doing well at Weybridge—her small sons were growing fast, as were Nick's.

Me, on the left of the table, on board the Aquitania, en route for England.

Harry meanwhile was surviving as a *soltero*. Having completed his work in Bogota (where he attended his first bullfight) he had returned to Peru and was now working from Lima. His friends kept him well entertained and he ably survived rounds of the hotels, clubs and the races.

Yes, he was enjoying himself and certainly hadn't lost his eye with a gun. He gleefully reported spending a very happy weekend upcountry with his friends hunting golden plover and quail—with impressive results. He wrote countless letters and certainly kept me well informed—perhaps a little *too* well?

The night before De Silva (Johnny) took us to the Cabana after-dinner, he gave us a darned good dinner with trout and vintage wines, then he said he had a surprise and took us to see the nightlife of Lima. We went to a low haunt, full of whores and all types of men—two whores were very good looking. Round the room were artistic photographs of nudes, big photographs about two-and-a-half feet high. We had a couple of beers there and then went home to bed.

HARRY TO ME, 8 AUGUST 1939.

But perhaps just to keep things straight, I should say something about Harry and me. Having lived with him for over ten years now I was well used to his—shall we say—'observations' regarding the opposite sex and how to deal with them. What's more, I like to think I gave him as good as I got … We were happy and really solid. He was loving and proud of me and I was delighted that everyone loved him and his 'correctness'. (If only they'd known!) We both had the same sense of style. So all appeared to be going to plan. Until …

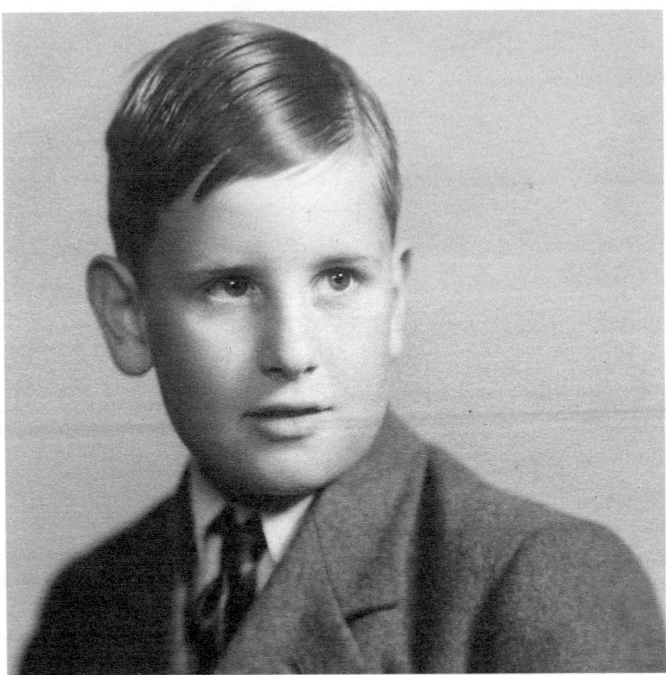

Alasdair in his school uniform.

Chapter 13
Wartime tussles

> So, war has come at last, God damn that bloody man Hitler. Darling I don't know what to think and it is so much more difficult as I have only had two of your letters from England. The one written on board and the second one sent via *Mauritania*. I expected a letter last week but didn't get one perhaps one will turn up tomorrow but unfortunately, I'm leaving tomorrow by air for Santiago and will not get it until Steve brings it by the next mail down. I'm wondering darling … if you have tried to get an earlier boat back, if you have thought of cancelling the *Queen Mary* and coming in an American boat. I am going to cable to you tomorrow suggesting you bring Alasdair out to Chile.
> HARRY TO ME, 3 SEPTEMBER 1939

The tranquillity of my stint in England came to a sudden halt on 3 September when we declared war on Germany. Harry was in Lima at the time and as Peru was sympathetic to Germany he *et al* beat a hasty retreat to Santiago. A few days later he was all togged up for Chilean Independence Day celebrations, on 18 September. A war wasn't going to obstruct matters like that: races, rodeos and agricultural shows—all carried on and required his presence.

Nevertheless, Harry was in a blue funk—well we both were. Letters took ages, some arriving weeks after others posted later. Harry's early optimism that it would somehow all blow over quickly vanished and the dilemma over what I should do grew

Harry and a colleague leave Peru as war breaks out, 1939.

and grew. Harry was desperate for me to return. And with all those dishy doxies around him in Santiago, so was I.

But if now, then how? Even if we could have afforded it, no aeroplane seats were available. And after the early sinking of the *Athenia* by a U-boat, everyone was scared.[3]

Harry insisted I take an American ship on the grounds that the Germans would not dare to sink one. Even then it would still be dangerous. On top of this there was a real risk that Harry might be recalled to England. We did our best to pull strings at the Air Ministry to find out but got nowhere; imagine me arriving in Chile just as he had been flown back to England.

And we didn't know what to do with Alasdair—bring him over or leave him behind in Brighton? In the event I took the plunge and, having landed in New York alone after a safe crossing on 5 December, I put myself back in the hands of Grace Line and sailed south, reaching Santiago just in time for Christmas. Would I have done the same if I'd known this was to be my base for the next three years?

Harry was in the pink. So were Wilfred and I. Life as a *soltero* hadn't been as tough as he had feared—a diet of tennis, picnics and clubs in and around Santiago kept him busy and he had had a merry time in mid-December when he flew up to Peru to parade along with his fellow attachés at the inauguration of President Prado at Lima on 8 December: the full diplomatic works he said. He made me rather jealous with his endless tales of *pachamanca* and other Peruvian food delights and the like, but what really mattered was that we were together again.[4] He was very relieved to have me back.

Coming back down to earth, one real fly in the ointment was that all the uncertainty and costs had led Harry to give up our home and lovely staff. So, I was promptly put in charge of

---

[3] U-30 sank the *Athenia* on 3 September 1939, having mistaken her for an armed merchant cruiser, triggering the Battle of the Atlantic.

[4] Traditional Peruvian meat dish baked in a pit lined with hot stones.

With friends and drinks at 2712 El Arrayán, our second Santiago home.

re-establishing ourselves in Santiago in a cottage he had found in a street called El Arrayán (house number 2712), which of course I did miracles with in my usual style.

We also had to get another car. Alasdair launched himself into 'advising' us at long range what to buy. You know, if he had put as much as half of his energy into his schoolwork, he might have been an exceptional scholar. His letters were not so much full of advice but endless 'instruction' and demands for photos; was nothing else happening in his life? It drove Harry crazy.

We quickly fell back into the old routine—dancing, friends, endless cocktail parties and adventures of one kind or another. We made a good team. I was the social organiser and (if I may say so) a brilliant hostess while Harry excelled as jovial host. He was in his element. His diplomatic duties seemed to revolve around entertainment of one kind or another. He was particularly pally with the Chilean air force, who arranged all kinds of events. There were grand luncheons to greet or say goodbye to fellow attachés and once in a while the womenfolk would be invited too. These events inevitably included group photographs in which Harry stands head and shoulders above the others. In or out of uniform, he looked magnificent—he always dressed beautifully. We had good friends who arranged fishing and shooting parties that were both productive and riotous. One weekend his Chilean counterparts took him out to a ranch where they had arranged for him to have a go at bullfighting. Hilarious—and somehow he emerged unscathed. Everyone loved us—thought we were the most glamorous couple. Life was good.

You know, while the lads indulged themselves with whatever tickled them at the time, we womenfolk had plenty to do. We all got on well, gossiped too much, drank excessively, and teased each other mercilessly. We held back no secrets from each other.

And the war? To begin with our situation was very odd. Not much happened—either in Chile or back at home. Even in Santiago we called it the Phoney War.

The war did not seem to reduce diplomatic pomp, although you could almost 'taste' the anti-British or anti-German feelings, depending on where you were. Of course, we kept clear of the local Germans—a bit tricky in diplomatic circles.

Harry has a go at bullfighting. Well, someone had to. (He survived.)

Once, Harry was horrified to realise that he had just shaken a Jerry's hand.

Fortunately, Alasdair's letters were mostly calm. It was almost as if he was locked in a world of his own. He was obsessed with his bike and quite fearless in the face of a pretty hard winter—no shortage of ice or snow to add to his excitement. And as for cars! His advice on what we should be driving rose to new and dizzy heights. He just couldn't stop. Drove us mad.

> Thank you very much for the airmail letter. A 1½ l S.S. [Jaguar] 1939 Saloon is being advertised for £195. There is no 1939 2½ litre, but a 3½ litre is £245. I have just seen a 2½ litre for £245. If you're going to get that it depends how much lower you can make the price. I think the tax for a car like that would be rather a lot. The Triumph had a very small tax compared with a car like that. How much do you think you will get for the Chevrolet if you have not sold it yet. When Mummy came over here last summer she said something about you thinking of getting a Humber Super Snipe and then selling it at once. We could have an MG. Only I am not very sure that I quite like those cars. An MG 18 hp (I think 2 litres, but I have forgotten) is being advertised for just over the SS 2½ litre price. We could even have a Triumph 16 hp. A [Triumph] 14/60 is being advertised for £195. There is no 16 hp one at all. The Hillman 14 are quite big enough (a new one) but they are not very fast. All they are supposed to be able to do is just over 70 mph (quite enough for Mama I expect!!!). I can't think of any more cars that we could have that would be of any use. American ones would have much too high a tax. Except a Ford. We could not have a 10 hp one and 22 would really be rather a lot. Anyhow I don't think we want a Ford at all. I think this is about all I can say concerning cars.
>
> (ALASDAIR TO MARGARET, 11 FEBRUARY 1940

And his fixation with detail didn't stop there. I remember him showing a rather macabre interest in the spread of German Measles around the school which he charted from letter to letter—apparently much more interesting than the war—but he may well have been more nervous than we thought.

> I had an awful dream last night. It was about myself being on a ship that was mined or torpedoed and I got into the sea instead of a lifeboat and found that I could not swim away from the ship. I can't remember after that. I don't think I got drowned.
> ALASDAIR TO MARGARET, 3 MARCH 1940

What was going on inside his head?

News from the rest of the family in England was calm so far. While we heard little from my siblings, Sylvia kept Harry up to date with their mother and was determined to stay on in London regardless of the war. And Daddy kept up with a steady stream of letters, topped up with missives from Mama. Apart from the small matter of 'managing' Alasdair and his bicycle and keeping him happy during the holidays, Daddy sounded quite relaxed and kept us up to date with my siblings, although he couldn't contain his criticism about Angela's family.

> You will be amused to hear that I started another correspondence in the *Sussex Daily News* on pacifism and have already written about four letters which means I have pleased some people and have had several letters of congratulations also an anonymous letter not threatening but apparently trying to convert us by argument! ... Michael came with Barbara just for the night of his birthday. I have not seen him looking so well since he left England to go to Rangoon. The relief from not having that long railway journey twice a day must be enormous. ...

Nicholas always writes whenever his ship gets back to port but his letters are not very interesting for the very good reason that he manages not to tell us any of the exciting news, which he has to keep bottled up.

Angela and Maurice are still living apart which I think is very bad and for them, entirely to his selfishness. ... I have come to the conclusion that he is thoroughly selfish and self-centred and I think it would do him a lot of good if his job was no longer reserved and he had to do his bit somewhere. I don't suppose he would be accepted for active service because of his deafness but I should like him to be given some really hard job in some uncomfortable surroundings to bring him to his senses.

DADDY TO ME, 22 MARCH 1940

What with him turning seventy, it was a good thing Mama was a relatively sprightly fifty-nine or so; he wasn't going to improve!

We were now well into 1940 and in March I joined Harry for an official visit to Bolivia centred on the inauguration of President Peñaranda in April. We went up the coast to Antofagusta en route to a nitrate mine at a place called Maria Elena. The reason that I remember it is that it was vast: I have never seen such huge machinery in my life, gobbling up, transporting and then crushing the minerals. On the way Harry had a go at deep sea fishing and caught his first dolphin. He was very pleased with himself.

Having flown up to La Paz from Arica we were swept up in what seemed like an endless round of parties, culminating in the inauguration itself. When I think about it now, the whole affair was wildly overblown. We stayed at the ambassador's house at the Delegation, where Sir Charles Bentinck, the ambassador, was a wonderful host. There were lunch parties, celebrations with the Bolivian air force and a hilarious get-together on an ancient steamer that plied Lake Titicaca—it had

Reed fishing boats on Lake Titicaca, on the border of Bolivia and Peru.

been made in England, brought to Peru in bits and then assembled on the lake shore.

Time seemed to have stood still on the lake—there were countless canoes (*balsas*) for fishing and what-have-you, made of reeds and the women wore the local equivalent of bowler hats. Heaven knows what they thought of us and our antics ...

Life had developed into a pattern. While 'home' was in Santiago, Harry was on the move to this country or that for much of the time and I joined him whenever this was possible. His beat stretched from Chile to Panama and we had some wonderful experiences up and down the Pacific coast.

The news from home just got worse as we crept further into 1940. France collapsed and England was now under threat. Both my brothers were now in uniform. We were relieved to hear that sailor Nick had emerged in one piece, having been on the battleship HMS *Warspite* throughout the Second Naval

Battle of Narvik on 14 April 1940. Meanwhile, brainy Michael was now an officer in the Army, hoping to be posted to Africa. We also heard that Barbara's brother, Cedric, Michael's boss, had been caught up in the retreat to Dunkirk, had been badly wounded and was now a prisoner of war in Germany.[5] Very frightening.

Talking of Dunkirk, we were proud to hear those two local paddle steamers—the *Brighton Belle* and the *Brighton Queen*—met glorious ends during the evacuation from the beaches. The *Belle* picked up 800 men, only to strike a submerged wreck on the way home. Happily, all 800 were rescued before she sank. The *Queen*, however, was dive-bombed and sank just offshore after picking up 700 French Moroccans, most of whom jumped to safety. Both these old leisure steamers had been pressed into Royal Navy service during the last war.

In the summer Harry and I left Santiago for what turned out to be an extended tour of Peru. After attending various diplomatic events and related festivities we took time for ourselves and toured the central highlands. This began with an extraordinary train journey that took us to a place called Huancayo, high up in the Central Andes. As we slowly made our way up from sea level we were treated with marvellous views as we zigzagged our way through the mountains, reaching around 16,000 ft at one point. There were flimsy bridges across the gorges that looked as though they were made of Meccano, tunnels and I don't know what else. The drops down to the valleys below were terrifying. But—what an experience. Somehow we coped well with the altitude.

When we reached Huancayo we found a town which was full of history and character—there was a monastery that we explored and was beautifully preserved. From there we descended a long way [about 8,000 ft] down a scary road to a

---

[5] Lt Col Cedric Odling, c/o of 140 Field Regt RA, was wounded during the rearguard defence of Cassel, in France, on 28 May 1940.

The seventeenth-century monastery of Santa Catalina at Huancayo.

place called San Ramon, which was almost tropical by comparison and where Harry had friends. They took us on to a valley inhabited by Perené peoples—a very small tribe who lived in a wildlife paradise.

Here I saw my first *Chunchos* Indians [isolated and rarely seen] who were strangely welcoming even though looking weird. After that everything seemed rather tame. We made our way back to Lima for the trip back to Santiago. And back to reality …

We missed Alasdair. He would have revelled in our Andean adventure, which we had told him all about. But he never commented on them. Was he silently angry because he was excluded? Or was his mind stuck in his own world and drama that was unfolding at home. And how did he *really* deal with the news that one of his friends' brothers had been killed in action?

I have not had a letter from you this week. I forgot to tell you last term that Henderson's brother's plane crashed. Mrs Henderson might have told. But if she has not you must not write to her. Because Henderson told Dean and Dean told me and Henderson was not meant to tell anyone. It happened last term only no one knew any details about it. This morning Dean told me that Henderson's brother was over Belgium in a Westland Lysander only it had so many machine gun bullets in it that it caught fire and crashed.

Gymnastics at St Andrew's, Eastbourne. Alasdair is in there somewhere.

The observer tried to pull him out but his hands and face were all burned awfully and no one is sure whether either of them escaped. He was the person who came down at half term and took me out with his mother and father.

ALASDAIR TO ME, 30 JUNE 1940

We couldn't work it out. But this was a poignant reminder of the relief—for me at least—that Harry was well away from the front line.

So—like it or not—we were stuck. Yes, Daddy and Mama had done brilliantly with their care for Alasdair but it was evident that they were sorely tried as the year dragged on. Our boy had been boarding at the Eastbourne prep school but, by May, the bombing had triggered an exodus of schools from the Home Counties to safer areas, and he ended up in Devon. That suited him: endless swimming and adventure and not much tuition. But I was concerned and disagreed with Harry that, on balance, it would build up his character and all that.

I didn't want to lose my other child, so we decided to try and get him to Chile. Complete nightmare. Cost, permissions, visas, safe ships (were there such things?), someone to escort him … We tried everything—pulled strings to get him a passport, even roped in Sylvia, who thought she could get him escorted to New York via a friend at the French Embassy. Mama jumped through hoops. And everyone (Daddy, Nick, the Air Ministry) said, 'Don't do it—much safer to stay here. Why not go to Scotland near Bunty?' By the end of the year we had given up and Alasdair was v. disappointed. He felt it was our fault. Or rather mine. He never missed a chance to have a go at me:

> Every week we have marks out of 15 for how hard the master of the class thinks we work. I forgot to tell you last time that I got 6/15 and this week 11/15 which was much better. The other day we were told that we would not be able to have as much tea as we used to have soon. So, we could either have milk, cocoa or coffee. I said I would like coffee. The chief reason … was because you never used to let me have it. But now you can't stop me! Ha ha! In a way it's your own fault: you once let me have it when we were at Wittering. Otherwise I would not have known that I liked it at all.
> ALASDAIR TO ME, 14 JULY 1940

It was as though I should have scooped him up when I left at the end of '39 …

Chapter 14
Angst and agony at home

I can't believe he is dead, or I couldn't if I hadn't gone to the funeral and seen that horrible little casket, which made me feel sick.
ANGELA TO ME, 20 JUNE 1942

Then the Battle of Britain began and with it came the bombing of the UK. Thank heavens, Highdown was far from the centre of Brighton and to my surprise the aged relatives were unusually relaxed about their own safety:

> I fear from your cable that you are very worried about Alistair and, owing to the difficulty of communication of course, we have been unable to let you know about our strenuous efforts to get your wishes carried out. Mama's letter will tell you all about it and I can assure you that ... she has worked like a horse on your behalf. I hope however you have become less worried yourself as the tragedy of the war has gradually unfolded. To begin with, now that the Empire is so to speak on its own and we know exactly where we are, everybody has got his tail up. Then, as to Alasdair, I hope very much that the Americans will decide to send ships to England to fetch the children and I would simply hate him to travel in a British ship because I believe the Germans would sink any British ship if they got the chance even though they knew it to be full of children. We had another air raid last night but no bombs; Mama will have told you about the bombs last week. Not very comfortable ... but I think you'd be surprised

if you knew how calm everybody is. Indeed, both Mama and I stop in bed when the warning's on and will continue to do so unless we hear bombs or guns going off. Food plentiful but financial matters of course very serious—more than half my own income gone at one fell swoop from loss of directorships and investments in my hotels. But nothing matters if the Almighty will give us victory.

DADDY TO ME, 23 JULY 1940

Mother maintained a steady monologue about the difficulties and possible dangers of getting Alasdair onto a ship and reminding us that, as far as she was concerned, our brushes with Chilean earthquakes and possible revolutions were 'small beer' compared with our big air attacks etc.

Alasdair, in his own way, was rather more deadpan:

I have kept on forgetting to tell you about Henderson's father. I expect you probably know actually.

Well anyhow he was posted in charge of Scotland's fighter command. Lots of things seem to have happened to the Hendersons in this war. Here in the holidays it is very nice. We bathe two or three times a day.

It's awful. I can't think of a single thing to say in this letter.

Your last letter was written from Lima. I hope you had a nice time there.

Granny said she may come down here, only now that I've got to go in an American ship, she said that it might be better if she stayed put in one place. I don't really see what it matters if the ship is American or British because the Germans sink any old ship that they can get hold of.

Yesterday we heard a lot of gun-firing out to sea. We don't know whether it was practice or a proper fight. I have forgotten which way to spell practise.

I hope you are very well. I am. Lots of love.

ALASDAIR TO ME, 17 AUG 1940

And, from Daddy:

> It looks as if we are going to be desperately hard up next year. I myself personally seem to be heading for a complete debacle as I will have to provide supertax as calculated on a very good year but charges at a time when our money bags are empty. And so, all we can do is send you fairly frequent airmail letters. Mama has told you all about Alistair. She has steadily toiled and tries to carry out your wishes so far as we know them and the Air Ministry are wanting to be most helpful but as she will have told you what with the uncertainty and what is available here everything is most difficult. As I told you, not only did the AM think you were unwise to have him out but also feel that the danger of the voyage outweighs the danger here, but your last suggestion that you and Harry might be recalled absolutely puts the lid on.
>
> Meanwhile I can assure you that everybody at home has his tail up. ... No doubt if we were to get bombed more frequently in Brighton we should not be quite so happy, but I must say the sound of them in the distance and the gunfire and the hundreds of aircraft zooming overhead are oddly exciting.
>
> Of course, the Germans talk about people cowering in their air raid shelters in absolute terror. ... Everybody looks perfectly normal and in between the warnings the streets are full of lively shoppers just as usual. We are rationed of course for meat and butter and sugar but the shops are so full of other good things that one does not note it at all. As for petrol I was allocated one extra gallon a month for the Minx on the pleas of my arthritis and the need of getting down to the hotels from time to time. Talking of hotels, I think the Old Ship must be keeping open without much loss but to my great grief I fear the Bedford is at its last gasp and will have to close.
>
> DADDY TO ME, 18 AUGUST 1940

You must be very worried by the news which reaches you, especially as to the safety of Alasdair. I may be wrong but I feel it almost providential that you … put a stop to all our efforts to embark the boy when you sent over instructions firstly that, if a British ship, then it must be convoyed and, later on, that on no account must it be a British ship. When you realise that he might have been on one of those torpedoed ships you must be feeling profoundly thankful. Safety in England anywhere nowadays is of course a comparative term but I really feel that the boy is now almost as safe as he would be ANYWHERE with the imminent prospect of America becoming involved. … You will have been horrified to hear about London & indeed the suffering of the poor Cockneys must have been too awful to think of, but after all the actual damage done is almost infinitesimal compared to the vastness of the city & it means that civilians are now in the front line. That being the case one calls to mind that we lost much more in a week from time to time in the last war than London has lost altogether.

DADDY TO ME, 8 OCTOBER 1940

And then a German plane machine-gunned Daddy while he was walking Moses, his dog, on the Downs. While he wasn't hit, he was scared out of his wits by the stream of bullets that thumped into the ground near him: the noise alone was terrifying. Alasdair wrote to tell us with great glee that it must have been a Junkers 89 'because that is the only 4-engined German bomber'.[6] He may have thought it was exciting, but I was terrified. Why couldn't the boy get it into his head that this was serious?

My dearest Peggy,
    We look forward very much to getting your letters and

---

[6] Author's note: Unlikely, as the only two JU89s built were reported as scrapped in 1939. More likely a Focke-Wulf Fw 200 Condor, perhaps.

are pleased to know that you are well and happy. By this time, I expect you got your Harry back to give you his comfort and protection and give you an opportunity to bully him from time to time after the custom of your Mama. So far, I am glad to say all the family are safe and well, but I wish Angela would send her boys to complete safety in Northwest Scotland.

They know nothing of air raid warnings or bombs where Bunty is living. They [Angela et al] have had a much quieter time lately at Weybridge but any day the Huns might start again in an attempt to destroy Vickers and Brookland's. Nicholas appears to be in Scotland and his ship seems to keep mainly in harbour. ...

Michael is having a quiet and eventful life near Lincoln. Mama keeps wonderfully well considering the life we lead and I am now ever so much better. Curious that I should have had such a severe [nervous] reaction coming on many days after my unpleasant adventure on the Downs. We constantly hear of the Huns machine-gunning civilians nowadays, but I must have been one of the first of their victims.

We lead an exciting and somewhat awesome life. Anything up to seven or eight air raid warnings a day and as soon as darkness falls (about 6:30 pm) a continual succession of bombers 'chug chugging' over the house on their way to London. Last night we heard about 20 bombs dropped in different directions; so far as I know at present, all outside Brighton; every day there are one or two, but it is wonderful how often they drop providentially on open ground, or empty houses, and what little harm, comparatively, [there has been] since the tragedy of the Kemp Town cinema with about 70 killed and 200 injured, mostly poor little kiddies.

DADDY TO ME, 7 NOVEMBER 1940

But indirectly, the bombing hit him fair and square. To be fair, he had done very nicely out of his hotels up until then, and the Army had already closed down the beach areas to store arms and ammunition. Not good for tourism. But the *Luftwaffe* killed it for a long time. I dare say that Brighton got off lightly compared with London, Liverpool, Southampton etc. but the bombs scared everyone away. Hotels closed *en masse*. Somehow Daddy's two clung on but income vanished almost overnight. What was worse, he and his fellow directors had spent a small fortune refurbishing the Old Ship not six months before.

> Tragic about London isn't it? I suppose Brighton is almost a paradise compared to it; but we seem to be getting the better of the Huns even there and no doubt as time goes on we will be able to perfect our defences. I could have cried with joy when the news of the American election came on the wireless, I have been praying Roosevelt might succeed. ... I expect you agree too that Roosevelt is a tower of strength to us and with his renewal mandate will be helping us more and more.
>
> Are not the Greeks doing wonderfully? If they can only continue to hold out I should not wonder if we were able to 'down' Italy within six months and that would be a full stage on the way to complete victory. I hope you never fail to pray hard for that happy day to come each day when as I feel sure that you do, you remember your own boy and your Mama, Papa and brothers and sister in your prayers. Fermor, our gardener, has gone off to join the air force and I'm going to try to manage with a man twice a week. There is luckily not much to be done just now and I am not much good nowadays. Talking of the air force, haven't they done wonders? Absolutely magnificent! We must not have any of that tragedy of demobilised officers tramping round trying to sell carpet sweepers etc. after the war. I think that all the money subscribed to buy spitfires ought to have been subscribed to an air force fund for disabled airmen. It is obviously a pure stunt.
>
> DADDY TO ME, 7 NOVEMBER 1940

What irony. Daddy had been so proud of his wealth, lifestyle and ability to support his children. Mama too, was devastated; income from her Trust Fund sagged and she was reluctant to raise money by selling stocks at a loss. Money (or rather lack of it) became a nightmarish recurring theme—house too expensive to run, staff reductions essential, endless search for economies and super-tax to pay (big, unending whinge). And—for us—the realisation that she might not be able to cover Alasdair's expenses (school extras, holidays, entertainment etc.). My fault of course. Mama gradually wound down her financial support, until in '41 she finally stopped the allowance she had given me since the year dot. If anything this made Harry's 'Scottish' approach to spending money (or rather *not* spending it) even more acute.

Mama's whingeing about all her 'hardships' never stopped: servants, 'all that housework', Jews, money and super-tax woes (along with eye-watering revelations about her private income), having to make do, shelling out for Alasdair and the endless accounts, Daddy and that 'wretched' dog Moses. The list was endless and her moans about lost letters, penny pinching and rationing—not forgetting endless gossip—ground me down.

> Do you realise that we have not been without a gardener for 14 years and not without a man (coachman or chauffeur) all our married days to cope with the boots and the boiler.'
> MAMA TO ME, 8 FEBRUARY 1941

And I was depressed by the constant 'dear Nicholas' vs 'poor Michael' slants in her letters. Somehow Nick could do no wrong and Mikey was a big disappointment. It was interesting to compare their obsession with Nick's promotion progress and his gong with their low-key reporting of Mikey's struggles).[7]

---

[7] Nicholas Copeman was awarded the Distinguished Service Cross for a 'special mission'—something to do with capturing a secret torpedo.

Daddy's letters were more positive. Unlike Mama (who generally refused to talk about the progress of the war but did manage to lament the sinking of the *Repulse* and *Prince of Wales*) Daddy took a great interest in the various campaigns and was delighted with the added information from the American papers that Harry sent him. Unbelievably he was convinced that we would win because 'we have God on our side.' He could be critical—was very unimpressed by Angela's husband Maurice and thought Mikey's wife Barbara 'dull in the extreme'. He was very unhappy about Angela and the boys—wanted them away from Weybridge and bombs. And he couldn't shake off his depression about his hotels and loss of income. To Mama's fury he was fiercely devoted to Moses who, aging steadily, became more and more infirm.

In the face of all this we were only too grateful for Santiago society: entertainments and some wonderful fishing trips. You know, the parties became more and more exotic; there was even one at Hector Buzo's gold mine!

We visited the workings after our lunch at Hector Buzo's gold mine.

Harry was still travelling a lot and made one more long trip that year, this time to Ecuador and Columbia. He never really let on what he was up to, but I'm sure that he was on the lookout for general information as well as all the strictly air-force-related stuff. After all, as in Chile, many of these countries were still stuffed with German expats. Aside from this he had one hell of a scare while in Bogota; his driver killed a drunk lurching along a dark road while Harry was on his way to a party. Blood everywhere, he said.

I don't remember much about it and I became a rather accomplished grass widow—gratifyingly never short of company. You know, somehow lust was always nearby in Santiago. Harry could get quite touchy about this in his letters. Very silly —I think it offended his vanity to think of other men being 'allowed' to admire me. This was so hypocritical—he was obsessed with his appearance and his looks. No wonder Alasdair inherited his fussiness over clothes. What is worse he could be cruelly disdainful about men or women that were plain or poorly dressed. He was particularly disrespectful of beautiful women who (in his opinion) wasted themselves on ugly men.

Well somehow we trundled on, although there were some real frights. The Jerries bombed and badly damaged Nick's ship in the Mediterranean during the Battle of Crete. He was one of the few officers who survived and he lost a lot of friends.

Sylvia worried us too—working at the Iraqi Legation during the day and serving as an air raid warden by night. We learned later that she was in London almost every night of the blitz in '40 and '41. Her tales of getting people into shelters during raids, looking out for more bombs and finding the dead and dying were enough to make anyone's hair curl.[8] Years later she told me that she still had her tin hat.

As far as our news was concerned, the family wasn't

---

[8] Almost 7,000 air raid wardens were killed during the Second World War.

remotely impressed by our tales of earthquakes, tornadoes, revolutions or Harry's severe car smash ('nothing compared with what we are suffering here!').[9] We did our best to send them goodies to ease the rationing pain, (Daddy being desperate for sugar and the women for dress material and silk stockings). There was endless correspondence about progress; whether the 'goods' would turn up, would be seized by customs or had been torpedoed. We couldn't help chuckling at Daddy's fright when the Customs threatened to seize a large bag of sugar that had arrived at Liverpool without the correct paperwork. He got Maurice to sort that one out for him.

But the smugness about their heroics with Alasdair was unbearable; 'you don't know how much we have tried to comply with his wishes'. And it didn't stop. Endless questions and complaints: 'what can we do about the holidays and how will we pay for it? His clothes? Which school should he go to next? 'Do try and persuade him that his prospects will be bleak if he doesn't start to take school more seriously? Otherwise, how will he pass the Common Entrance exam?'

Well, what with parents scrapping about this as well, we had to face this head-on and in the event we settled on Wellington College (realising too late that he could have got into Charterhouse as 'required' by Mama which—by the way—would have saved us a lot of money).[10] Anyway, he did pass the entrance exam when the time came, so Wellington it would be.

---

[9] Harry was in Bolivia during the attempted coup of 1940 and the Guayaquil earthquake in Ecuador of May 1942.

[10] Charterhouse School, at Godalming in Surrey since 1872, was established in the 1600s and is one of the 'great' nine English public schools reported upon by the Clarendon Commission in 1864. Margaret's brother Michael was at Charterhouse, Alasdair was offered a place, and bursaries were available. Wellington College, at Crowthorne in Berkshire had very strong military links and Margaret's mother disapproved. Angela's husband Maurice was at Eton: their sons would go there.

Christmas 1940 came and went. We endured a very stuffy British trade mission and compensated ourselves with another trip south to Pucon and the lakes and lots of fishing. I even became quite keen myself.

In '41 Harry was upped to group captain and full-blown air attaché. From time to time he would disappear on trips to other British missions and who knows what military intrigue. But he kept on writing. His letters were still full of outrageous language and revelations about visits to dubious establishments and who was poking whom; but full of love for me even if he still called me an 'old faggot'—the monkey. He also did his best to get me to cut down on my drinking while he was away. I must admit that he did have a point …

While he was away on one of his trips Daddy wrote, to my great dismay:

> This evening I had a most extraordinary letter from Cmdr. Locker-Lampson MP asking for a subscription towards the Jewish hospital in Jerusalem. He apparently thinks I am a Jew for he begins the letter, after saying how much he has been stirred by the tragedy of the Jewish people, as follows: 'while not a member of your great race, I think I realise perhaps as much as any Jew how your people have enriched civilisation' et cetera et cetera! How on earth came he to make such a bloomer? I am thinking of writing back to say that while I agree with him in my regret that the Jews should be tortured and persecuted as they have been, I have been equally shocked to see what bad citizens they are showing themselves to be in countries where they seek refuge, as here in England. Day after day the papers are full of reports of prosecutions of people for running gaming halls, questionable nightclubs and black markets and in nearly every case the defendants are described as Moses this or Aaron that. The decent superior Jews seem to do

nothing to check them or to sound out to them the rottenness of their behaviour.

DADDY TO ME, 18 OCTOBER 1941

As Mama reported it: 'AMC just fainted at the suggestion by Locker-Lampson that he was a Jew; replying 'it would be harder to find anyone of more proudly Aryan stock'.[11]

I was rooted to the spot. I was used to a steady stream of digs about Jewish people but this was far worse. Suddenly everything fell into place—great heavens, I was slow. I had never really understood why both she and Daddy had disliked Horace; now I realised: they thought he was Jewish and had somehow managed to keep this to themselves. But suddenly the cat was out of the bag. As if being a 'Goldsmith' meant that he must be Jewish ... and even if he was? How could they think like that? Did they sympathise with the dreadful stories now trickling out from Nazi Germany? And once Mama had started, she wouldn't stop. Not long afterwards she complained that a young Jewish boy called Christopher Copeman had joined Alasdair's school and was 'bubbling over with wrath at their daring to take over such a good East Anglian name'.

It was around this time that postal delays became almost impossible to bear. Literally months could go by without a peep from home. Very distressing. It caused confusion at home too.

My dearest Peggy
>
> We are getting very concerned about your letters. We are quite sure you do write to us more or less once a week, but it is now many weeks since we heard from you. ... There's certainly something very wrong, especially in view of the improved position in the Atlantic.

---

[11] Commander Oliver Stillingfleet Locker-Lampson, C.M.G., D.S.O. (1880–1954) was a British politician and naval officer.

We have had your boy here for two weeks and poor Mama now feels she has parted with her favourite child now that he has returned to school. He looked awfully fit and very huge and evidently enjoyed himself here. The only thorn was the very unsuitable way in which Grand Pops occupied every possible opportunity to press the importance of his work and school to fit himself for the many difficult times ahead. Grandpa is very wanting in fact; I expect he thinks! I feel sure he has plenty of brains if directed in the proper direction, but I fear motor cars and aeroplanes leave him little time and energy for discussing such unimportant subjects as mathematics, classics et cetera. It might be well if Harry would write and point out to him what a bleak world was likely to be for boys who have not been well educated and so fitted to fill government and other administrative jobs. Mama and I are really wonderfully well considering all our anxieties. …

We seem to be slowing up the Japs a bit in Malaya. I always had a feeling that the Huns would not get into Leningrad or Moscow and now I have the same feeling that we will hold Singapore all right. By the time you get this we ought to know for certain one way or another. But we and the Americans seem to have known very little of the vast preparation made for attack on us and to have misjudged their strength and their ability. I am hoping and praying we may soon be able to down Rommel for good in Libya and so relieve lots of men and material for other campaigns.

DADDY TO ME, 26 JANUARY 1942

Mama's grumbles rumbled on: no, they got worse:

… why don't the authorities stop all professional football, all horse racing, all dog racing—scandalous they should be allowed to go on. I think a little euthanasia for lunatics, the helpless, the perverts and hardened criminals & all old things over 90 might also ease up food, attendants, clothes, lighting & heating and various other necessities.

MAMA TO ME, 12 FEBRUARY 1942

Alasdair's imminent shift to Wellington didn't help either. He needed new clothes—tricky because of rationing, let alone the cost. And she still couldn't resist reminding me that we really should have chosen Charterhouse. She was mad at me because I was short of cash and her irritation at having to sell off securities cheaply to settle my bills was plain. Harry's failure to arrange Alasdair's school fees just made things worse. Enough said, I suppose.

In spite of all this, news from England kept us grounded—we just had to know what was going on. Daddy, bless him, managed to keep up his optimism most of the time:

> I expect you are both worried by the early successes of the Japs and it is evident that their strength was grossly underestimated, just as we also failed to recognise that if they could get advantage by gross treachery they would certainly do so. The loss of Singapore was a grievous blow and it does not look as if Java has much chance, but things are brighter in Burma and if we can hold on there a time must come soon when the difficulties caused by their tremendously long chains of communication will begin to find out weak spots for us to attack. ... But meanwhile it must be beastly for you reading the news and finding nothing but excuses for disaster after disaster. We cabled you this morning to tell you Alasdair has passed the common entrance for Wellington, so there is a small drop of better news for you.

DADDY TO ME, 5 MARCH 1942

We were well aware of the disasters in the Far East. But where was Toby? As an RAF reservist he had been sucked into the chaos of Malaya and Singapore but we knew no more than that. We had heard from Irene, his wife. She was safe, having managed to escape from Singapore to Australia, but was equally confused. We had no idea where Toby was, or even whether he was alive or not.[12]

By early 1942 we knew at last that Harry would not be recalled for 'active' service; he was too old and his flying skills were by now completely out of date. He was also unwell. Having struggled with haemorrhoids for some time, he finally had surgery to sort them out. He recovered in the spring just to begin what was to be his last long trip—Columbia, Ecuador and Peru, I think.

This was not without incident: I remember being scared out of my wits when I heard of a severe earthquake in Ecuador that killed about 300 people.[13] It was ages until I learned that although Harry was 250 miles away in Quito, the Legation building shook so badly that he had to get everyone out into the garden. Guayaquil was badly clobbered but he was safe—and definitely back to normal when, true to form, he wrote from Lima:

> Last night I had dinner with an alleged Nazi agent (an Argentine), met and spoke to the blonde spy—finished up for some eats with a Peruvian woman (about 24 years old and damned good looking) and her husband (both quite respectable!). The beauty is to be at the Argentine embassy tonight so I am naturally going to make a pass at her which of course I can do as I have met her once or twice before!!

---

[12] Toby, then an RAF Flying Officer, escaped from Singapore only to be caught and imprisoned by the Japanese at Boei Glodok PoW Camp, Java in 1942. He was moved to another camp near Batavia [Jakarta] in 1943 and remained there for the rest of the war

[13] The Guayaquil earthquake occurred on 13 May 1942.

Thousands more kisses, you needn't worry about the Peruvian. Your most adoring Harry

HARRY TO ME, 25 MAY 1942

He wasn't to know it but his joking coincided with some dreadful news that I had to weather on my own until he came home a few days later. Mikey had died at the end of March following surgery that had gone wrong. He had been in a hospital in Yorkshire and in great pain. They classed it as 'death on active service'. What was worse, the news didn't reach me for a couple of months. Damn the post.

I hesitate to say this but I think Mama was more angry than sad—though this may be a bit harsh when I recall that we both knew how hard it was to bury one's own child. Not normal. As she reported:

Operation for intestinal obstruction—though 'critical'—he was bearing up. B[arbara] sat with him till he died soon after midday on 21st. We arrived too late. He was in pain, had very little attention (except for a parson's visit), but was conscious, & until near the end, very confident of recovery, poor old darling. Then Barbara saw he realised it was not to be. Father was furious that a local surgeon in a tiny country infirmary dared to undertake such a major operation when less than 20 miles away was Leeds, with the best men in England. 'Adhesions from the operation causing a kink in the bowel—hence the stoppage.' We saw him in the chapel but we came home early Monday as he had wishes to be cremated.' Small service with ashes at Hove cemetery. Reggie & Gladys, Angela, Mrs Od., several members of the firm and some 2 dozen wreaths from brothers, sisters, army friends, the firm.'

MAMA TO ME, 20 MARCH 1942

Angela was sweet. She wrote much more thoughtfully and

explained further. They cremated him up in Leeds and she hated the horrid ceremony when they buried his ashes at Brighton. She was furious that *finally* people took notice of him. Me too. God, the hypocrisy ...

Eventually, the missing letters and parcels began to dribble in—months late.

Dearest Peggy.

Just a line to add to Mama's news and to confirm that all things considered we are both wonderfully well. My newly started food factory has done wonders for me in keeping my mind occupied and not allowing me too much leisure to brood over the awful catastrophe which has come upon us. Mama will have told you all there is to be told and how bravely poor Barbara is bearing her grief and facing a very hopeless future. We loved having Jeremy with us and I am glad to say, seeming to have done him a lot of good. He is a very dear little boy. As for your son he is growing up almost beyond recognition and I am proud that one serious talk with him about the difficulties of his future in the post-war world really seems to have had so much good effect as proved by the wonderfully improved report he brought home. He is very bright, a picture of health and evidently looks forward to going to Wellington. Mama has sought refuge for her broken heart by even more devoted service to the boy than ever and that is as you know saying a lot. ... You could not possibly provide any greater loving services to the boy than does his granny in your absence. I constantly ask him whether he realises what a lucky boy he is in that respect and I am sure he does. As a result, loves his granny very dearly. I am so glad you are both now so well but can understand how worried you must have been so far away not only from your son. ... But never fear—all will come brighter in the end. Ever so much love to you both.

DADDY TO ME, 28 APRIL 1942

There was a wonderful moment when I thought Mama's sense of humour had returned.

> Your letter was quite cheerful for a doting grass widow and groans about flu and 'the rifling of the Embassy bag by the local Gestapo'. Angela 'revelling in your floral silk dress'. Thinks that Customs have it in for Maurice (parcels not getting through). 'I should love to see you in the black [dress] cum diamonds & so feel very sure the effect is quite stately and does Britain credit.'

MAMA TO ME, 15 MAY 1942

And she even told Alasdair to make his letters more interesting for us—'no comments on your cars etc.'. Our parcels went down well too: 'your father will wallow in the butter & the sugar'. 'You would smile to see me queue up for three pennyworth of bullseyes or toffees.'

Soon after we heard that Alasdair had settled in well at Wellington. In the wake of Mikey's death and Mama's endless carping about getting him kitted out, what should have been joyful news somehow lost its gloss.

From his letters to us, it sounded as though he had faced the challenges of starting school head on: finding his way around, new boys tests, fagging etc. But unlike the dread of many of his fellow new-bugs, he did at least have the hang of wrestling with a shirt collar which had to be attached by studs to the shirt; Harry was amused.

But Alasdair was not remotely amused that as far as Wellington was concerned, he was 'Reid' and his protests about being 'McLaren-Reid' met with outright instruction 'no swank over the McLaren to be allowed.' He became very sensitive about the taunts, which went on for ages; and of course, it just added to his list of complaints about us.

Somehow Daddy managed to stay cheerful in spite of the

vagaries of the post.

My dearest Peggy

Such a spend of letters from you lately and even a wonderful parcel, the contents of which are a joy to me. Bad luck having to be a grass widow for so long but you sound cheerful all the same and evidently have lots of friends to share your loneliness. You and Harry must be feeling very bucked at the success of the RAF; indeed, the news all round is much more pleasing even if doing in the Libyan struggle still seems some way off. ... All goes well here—no bombs (touch wood) closer than Patcham [a mile or so away], but we are rather overworked trying to keep in the garden and look after the chickens. ...

We have had a letter from [Cedric] Odling from a camp in Germany expressing his tremendous sorrow at the 'loss of a very close friend' ... 'in whom all his plans were centred' ... 'for those brain power he had the greatest of respect.' Very charming but of course it rather reopens the wound. I'm so glad that Alistair obviously likes his life at Wellington—he simply can't believe that half the term is already over—and that he is now a boy scout. He is rather ominously silent about work, but I hope there may be a half term report presently ... I do do hope this (I fear) uninteresting epistle may reach you. It seems so absurd to be writing letters which never reach you. The weather after a week of almost intolerable heat is now pretty cool, but still Mama goes to Weybridge for a week on Sunday.

DADDY TO ME, 10 JUNE 1942

Mama's attention however switched to Barbara; how were she and her two young sons going to cope without Michael? '(If only Mrs O[dling] had not been such a poisonous female it would be really nice for them to live in comfort together here, but no one has a good word for Mrs O. She is so egotistical & self-centred, & hard at core, that Barbara could not possibly be

with her long.' And on top of Mama's revelation that she had paid for Mikey's funeral as 'we can't bear for his little estate to be depleted & have said we will pay for the memorial,' Barbara found out that she was not going to get a pension.

Casting aside the money moans, perhaps I should have been a wee bit more sympathetic; after all, she was getting old (or, at least, thought she was).

And to give her credit, both she and Daddy were very careful not to let Alasdair know about our various scrapes (car accidents, earthquakes and what have you).

Somehow, we all calmed down over the summer. Alasdair's first report was excellent and his long visit to friends in Scotland reduced tension at Hove. Harry was desk bound and

A formal dinner in Santiago, June 1942. Harry is circled.

had little to fret over apart from all the speeches he had to give at the various functions that preceded our departure—although we had no idea when.

Around this time Mama remarked that my letters sounded rather 'pianissimo' and (rightly) surmised that I wanted to come home. It was time. And I had had enough of postal delays, parental sniping, grass-widowing and the whole Alasdair saga. It was all very well for Harry: he had his work to keep him busy. Somehow, I thought that it was me who had taken the brunt of all the problems that had come our way. And I was afraid that Alasdair would drift away from us. So I was mightily relieved when Harry's recall date finally came (after many false alarms) and after a 'last fling before return to serfdom' he and I left for New York where we boarded the

Cunard liner *City of Exeter* and landed at Liverpool on 26 November 1942. The family was cock-a-hoop when we returned—Alasdair full of glee. But this didn't last for long ...

Looking back on it, despite all the trials and tribulations I think we would both agree that we had been in some of the most beautiful—and varied—countries on earth. Apart from the stunning scenery we had seen spectacular wildlife and some incredible peoples. Never to be forgotten. Do you know, I didn't manage to take a decent photograph of the mountains in all that time ...

Charles Orde, the ambassador in Santiago, later wrote a rather charming letter to the foreign secretary about Harry:

> This officer made himself very popular with Chileans generally and in particular with the Air Force. He also cultivated with great success relations with United States citizens, both official and unofficial, in Santiago. In both directions he was assisted to an exceptional degree by Mrs McLaren Reid. He was most helpful to me at all times and I was sorry to lose him from my staff.
>
> CHARLES ORDE TO ANTHONY EDEN, 11 FEBRUARY 1943

And so I was 'mentioned in despatches' as well!

Yet when I come to think of it, it really was time to come home. We both felt that somehow after all the razzamatazz of the past three years we had to get to grips with what was going on in England. You know, he never mentioned it, but I did wonder whether Harry quietly regretted that he hadn't been of more direct use to the war effort.

And would Alasdair forgive us?

Chapter 15
Marking time—the war

> [Alasdair] seems to have 'kept his head down' and
> not taken part in sport or other aspects of College life.
> There was one reference to him failing an exam in
> the Corps, so perhaps he was not very enthusiastic
> about that either!
> WELLINGTON COLLEGE ARCHIVES, JAN 2024

The rest of the war in Europe is rather a blur. We finally docked in Liverpool in late November '42 and headed straight off to a fine welcome at Brighton from two frail parents and an extremely fragile Moses. Alasdair was allowed to come home for a few days and we soon re-established ourselves at Hove. It was not as though I didn't recognise him, but his voice was beginning to break and he'd grown enormously. Harry hadn't seen him for well over four years. It was an emotional moment for all of us.

At some point Harry had to return to work and thankfully, rather than pack him off to Scotland or somewhere equally ungodly, the Air Ministry sent him back to play with experimental aircraft at Farnborough—this time flying a desk. So, we were soon on the move again and rented a house in Farnham called 'Homemead' that suited us very well. The office was only eight miles away and we were now much closer to Mayfair and its high life (or at least its war-time ghost) when we could afford it. Wellington College was only about 15 miles away.

The problem was that Harry had been away for four years

—he barely recognised his son. Harsh reality reigned—no money, rationing, grim clothes and increasing hostility from Alasdair who thought we were selfish and fickle. Also, I could tell the old adventurer was restless: in Latin America he had been a big cheese but now even group captains were ten a penny.

The funny thing was that we were closer than ever. We understood each other and our whims and fantasies only too well—birds of a feather you might say. Despite everything else Harry was calmer and strangely optimistic. At last he knew that I wouldn't run away. Silly boy.

I think Alasdair sensed and resented this closeness. Harry's relationship with him was very odd. The boy wanted to please. He valued Harry's advice, but I think felt sore that we were nowhere as rich as the parents of many of his school friends. So, it was a relief that he was away at school for much of the time; the pressure was off then and it was too easy for us to procrastinate about it. I suppose that it didn't help that Harry and I reacted in different ways: while I was hurt about it and the related flak from my parents, Harry was more frustrated that he and the boy seemed to have so little in common (apart from some expensive tastes). This rankled.

Thank goodness, we found that people still loved us and that there was still fun about despite the war. As for the family, we caught up with Angela and Bunty, but found that Barbara had somehow hidden herself away. We often saw Sylvia, who had emerged from the blitz unscathed and—foot loose and fancy free in her mid-thirties—was enjoying life in London in something of a devil-may-care way. We did our best to keep up to date with her on-and-off engagements—well, she certainly scooped up some very impressive men.

We managed to visit Harry's mother in Scotland once or twice—true to form, she was terrific company even if she did have the odd dragon moment. At Hove, we struggled with Mama's endless scraps with Papa and their endless gloom about servants and their investments. *And* advice on how we should handle Alasdair. And Toby: at last we heard that he was alive but cooped up in a PoW camp in Java. There were dreadful stories about the way that the Japanese treated their prisoners. Would he survive? Awful. Goodness knows what Bunny was going through in Australia.

Alasdair's obsession with motor cars and clothes-fussiness mushroomed. I wondered if he was trying to keep up with Harry. But were these more intense interests blocking out others? For example, he didn't seem at all interested in girls; in fact he didn't really show much interest in other people at all. Apart from racing around on his bicycle, he wasn't remotely keen on sport.

Harry simply couldn't understand this: the lad was so big and strong but took no interest in sport or 'manly' things. In contrast, Daddy and Mama thought him such a wonderfully rounded and delightful young man. Drove Harry mad ...

As far as school was concerned, he gave us the impression that he did his best to be invisible. We worried about his erratic academic progress and whether he would get good enough exam results to survive in the big wide world. Latin seemed to be his most successful subject at school, or at least the one that he found easiest—hardly not what Harry thought of as useful. Thank heavens, he managed to pull out all the stops and scrape through exams when it mattered.

Fortunately, there was never any question of Harry returning to operational service. He spent the last two and a half years of the European war managing experimental and testing programmes at Farnborough, much like his work in the early '30s but at arm's length as far as flying was concerned. I remember he was involved in research on wireless systems, gunsights and aerial photography, including some pretty inspirational stuff. But in truth, he found no fun in administration per se ...

There were few opportunities to fly and on 25 April 1944, he took up a Tiger Moth for his last flight. By then he had racked up over 2,000 hours in something like sixty different aircraft types and had distinguished himself operationally in four countries. Not bad.

And—let's be positive—we were in as safe a place as any in the southeast of England and I think that he had found unexpected peace within. You know, I think that his 'escape' from the operational mess of the war had somehow softened him—freeing him from the causes of his earlier aggression, tensions and anxieties. I'm sure that I was a very good influence on him. He finally began to believe in our stability and feel secure. He was content. And probably far less ambitious. We were a good team. And he was very cuddly ...

During one of our trips to London, Sylvia introduced us to an American who had been appointed to a naval position there and had invited us to lunch at Rules, just off the Strand. His name was Alan Davis, a career sailor—just like Nick. Alan had really done his homework; while the cost of the meal was limited to the statutory maximum of five shillings a head, this restaurant had access to abundant game which was off-ration and we ate (and drank) like kings and queens; a huge treat in wartime terms. They had reinforced the building with timber outside to provide protection during the blitz, but this did not detract from the quite magnificent interior.

After the drear of Farnborough life it was wonderful to see such a happy sister-in-law. She looked wonderful, was clearly smitten and the pair of them just hummed. It didn't take her long to decide to marry him.

Around this time we learned that Cedric (Barbara's brother) was back in England. Now forty-eight, he had been repatriated from his German PoW camp through some Red Cross scheme on account of his injuries in 1940. He was still a lieutenant colonel and they transferred him to SHAEF [Supreme Headquarters Allied Expeditionary Force] in Grosvenor Square, for what turned out to be the rest of the war. While the Odlings naturally were delighted, I found it both ironic and sad that he had survived and that Mikey—he whom Cedric saw as his successor at Anselm Odling & Sons—had not.

Otherwise time just passed by. Perhaps we measured its passing in terms of Alasdair's school calendar—events there, holidays, days out and what have you. One could feel that the tide of the war was turning—Sicily, D-Day, progress on the eastern Front and in the Pacific. Optimism rose. January 1945 came and went. We all believed the war was coming to an end and that some sense of normality would return. Some chance.

Alasdair (circled) and The Picton, Wellington College, 1944.

Chapter 16
Final fling?

> Wilfred and I both send our love and I hope we
> will get together again soon. There is a possibility
> that we might be together by September in Cairo,
> wouldn't that be just marvellous.
> Goodnight sweetheart, your own Harry
> HARRY TO ME, 21 JUNE 1945

Mediterranean mayhem

Well, VE Day came at last.[1] We drank all the Champagne we could find and licked our wounds. As for the family score card, we were still alive, Alasdair and the rest of the family, too—well almost ... Mikey was dead. We knew that Toby was rotting in a Japanese PoW camp and could only hope he was still okay. Mama and Daddy were hanging on, after a fashion, even though (in their not-quite-as-cosy-as-usual life) they thought they were 'penniless'; they little understood how most people managed on far, far less. But Mama was increasingly frail. At

---

[1] VE Day (Victory in Europe Day) was on 8 May 1945. It marked the official end of the Second World War in Europe, following Germany's unconditional surrender to the Allies on 7 May 1945. Victory over Japan Day (VJ Day), marking the end of the war in Asia and the Pacific, is recognised by two other dates: August 15, when Japan announced its surrender (observed as VJ Day in the UK and many other countries); and September 2, the date of the signing of the official surrender document aboard the USS *Missouri* in Tokyo Bay (recognised as VJ Day in the USA).

times we struggled to handle Alasdair. He was learning to be bolshy.

On the plus side, the first three years of the war had been a pretty good romp and Harry had managed to steer clear of any action; Nick was a hero; and Maurice was his usual boring old self. (God knows how or why Angela put up with him, but their children were fine and got on well with Alasdair.)

Then guess what? Harry's lords and masters decided to remind him that variety was indeed the spice of life and packed him off to a place near Naples. Still, they didn't put him out to graze like so many of his friends, so at least there was something to prop up the bank account every month. And I believed him when he said he had had enough of separation.

And so began a chaotic three years or so, ending with Harry's retirement from the RAF. For most of this time I felt like the filling in a very unappetising sandwich, with Harry on top and family struggles below. Ugh … .

Before Harry left, we packed up Homemead and took on a house in Salisbury Road, back in Hove again. This was fine, except that we had a real ding-dong with the Farnham landlord over alleged breakages that dragged on for about a year.

We had just two weeks of European peace before Harry was back in an aircraft and on his way to Italy. He managed to squeeze in a few very comfortable days in Paris on the way before reaching Caserta, a city about thirty miles north of Naples. With an office in the Royal Palace that was now the official residence of the big boss of the armies in Italy, General Sir Harold Alexander, Harry was back in his element—schmoozing with the Great and the Good in the name of inter-air force liaison.

> The minister's cocktail party was pretty good although according to our standards a small one. Alexander and all the other big shots were there. The minister reminded me

irresistibly of Bentinck.[2] I hear that the Lee-Smiths are still at the Vatican so I shall look them up on Tuesday next ... I have now counted the steps up to our offices—there are 205 and the lift was out of order today. From the top there is a very fine view—towards the north an avenue leads up to a waterfall which spurts out from half-way up the mountain, to the south down another avenue of huge trees, four deep, which must be some four miles long and dead straight. Before we took over the Palace it was the Cranwell of the Italian Air Force.

HARRY TO ME, 26 MAY 1945

As a place to live, poor dear, he thought it a real dump. He was back to living under canvas, with no booze ration for ages and feeling glum. But it didn't take him long to make friends, particularly of the female variety, and he did manage trips to Athens and elsewhere in the region. And, would you believe it, the old rascal celebrated his arrival with the award of a 'mention' for his efforts at Farnborough; how *did* he wangle that?[3]

Then came a flicker of hope: he might move on to Cairo and there was the exciting possibility that I might join him. Gradually the 'possibility' became a 'likelihood', which began with a tour of the Eastern Mediterranean that pulled in Cairo.

I will now finish telling you about Greece. Yesterday, the air commodore (Edwards-Jones with whom I flew back) and I went to see the Acropolis, which was well worth a visit. After that I met Willis Rees and had drinks with him, his wife and another woman at the Grande Bretagne hotel. His

---

[2] Victor Cavendish-Bentinck C.M.G. (1897–1990) was UK ambassador at Santiago, 1933–39.

[3] 'Mentioned in Despatches' is a term used to denote a member of the armed forces who has been commended by name in an official report to a senior officer.

wife is certainly very good looking and I should say about 32 years old. In the evening E-J and I took the others out to dinner at a small restaurant on the sea front. This is the only time we have been allowed to pay for anything. Although we had ordered lobsters there weren't any, so we had a red mullet instead—very good. AVM Darvall was with us as he had just arrived from Bucharest, bringing a huge tin of caviar which we polished off. The Russians are supplying a lot of it but at a high price, this tin cost £5. It is a damn shame that I should be telling you all this my beautiful when you can't be here to enjoy such things with me. On the other hand, you wouldn't like to have to live here in Naples much.

HARRY TO ME, 19 AUGUST 1945—FROM CASERTA

Meanwhile I held the fort, sent him supplies of Scotch and cigarettes and did my best to cheer him up at long range. This went on for around three months—just about bearable—and then Harry was finally posted to Cairo having already had a grand tour of the eastern Med.

Next morning, we started off for Cairo from Athens and arrived at 2:30 PM, had a drink in the mess and then went to Shepherd's for lunch where rooms had been booked for us. Cairo was hot and very sticky and the bedrooms (I shared with Dickie) stuffy and full of most annoying flies. The first night, Van Wyck, one of my officers and his wife, a very nice ugly woman, asked Olive and myself to dinner at Maia House. It was a quiet night there, but the dinner was excellent.

The next night the Van Wycks had a party for me at their flat. There were about 15 people and we had a very nice buffet supper, a dance or two and lots to drink—rather in the style of a small party in Chile. The next night E-J and I asked the Van Wycks, Olive and SASO's PA to dinner at the Auberge des Pyramides which is a new place on the way to the pyramids. As soon as you get out here, we will go to this auberge—you will love it as there is good food, a good band and a good dance floor … On Friday morning we left for Jerusalem and stayed there two nights with the AOC Palestine in his villa. It is 3,000 feet above sea level, so the climate was marvellous.

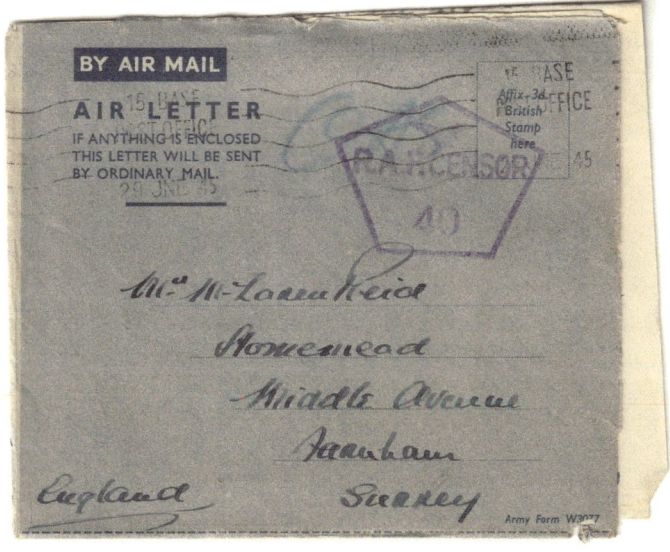

We did the usual sightseeing—the wailing wall, Bethlehem, the manger etc. and also bathed in the Dead Sea. Bathing in the Dead Sea was most peculiar, one just sat in it and it felt like being in a deck chair. When one tried to swim, one's feet floated so high that they kicked the air instead of the water!

Standing vertically, which was very difficult to do, I floated with the water level just above my titties but that wasn't for long because my feet then shot up and stuck out of the water. The AOC Palestine has a really grand job and does it very well. When we arrived at Lydda some 40 miles from Jerusalem, we were met with three aeroplanes, a Spitfire, a Miles Monitor and a Beechcraft. The AOC flew himself in the Spitfire, the Monitor took our luggage and E-J, Olive and I and the AOC's PA went on in the Beechcraft.

Dickie and the other Wing Commander had by this time left our party and are coming back independently. We all arrived together at a small aerodrome near Jerusalem which looked like a private flying ground, everything was spotlessly clean and the AOC's Chrysler with chauffeur and RAF policeman as footman waiting to take us up to the villa. Alistair would have liked the Chrysler which was a 7-seater, black and lots of chromium.

HARRY TO ME, 10 SEPTEMBER 1945

Harry's job in Cairo was to run a team called AFALS (Allied Forces Air Liaison Service), his 'empire' as he called it, and suddenly there was the prospect of joining him. We were both excited, little expecting to slide onto the roller-coaster of hope and disappointment that blighted the next eleven months—and ended, I now confess, in tears.

Harry's knack of falling on his feet didn't fail him. He wound up at all the fashionable places in Cairo—Shepheard's Hotel, parties given by diaspora royals, trips to the pyramids and fishing in the Gulf of Suez, not to mention official receptions here and there plus endless cocktails. As usual his eye for pretty young women didn't fail him either but I still believe that he never strayed beyond our mutually agreed limits.

VJ Day came and went. While I joined in the celebrations at home, Harry reported that the whole thing had been a damp squib in Cairo: the mood music had changed and there were rumblings:

> The end of the Second World War saw Egypt a great deal richer than she had been at the beginning. ... Yet all this money was going into the hands of the rich rather than the

poor. Prices had gone up by at least two-thirds since 1939 and showed no sign of descending, while wages had lagged behind ... So ... the immediate post-war years saw a period of painful change in Egypt.

ARTEMIS COOPER ON CAIRO LIFE AFTER 1945
CAIRO IN THE WAR 1939-1945, P.325

Then out of the blue we heard from Bunny that Toby was alive and that they were to be reunited in Singapore. Next thing they were on a ship and Harry just managed to catch it at Port Said as it emerged from the canal. Quite marvellous—they hadn't seen each other for years.

Harry was overjoyed. Contrary to our fears and expectations, Toby looked fit and well, but Harry couldn't get a word out of him about his ordeal, and Bunny was haggard. Awful ... I had the same reaction when I eventually caught up with the pair in London.

As for *our* predicament, somehow the ghastly confusions and fears of 1939 and 1940 were only too understandable: there was, after all, a war on and we feared losing one another.

But this post-war muddle was different. We were victims of a system that seemed to change from day to day, raising our hopes time and time again and then dashing them. As far as I could see, it was bloody useless.

What with worries about cost, luggage and 'rules' etc. that would have taxed the most patient soul, poor Harry did his level best to get me out to Cairo (where the colonial era hung on by its fingertips):

> The British still sipped their gin slings on the terrace of Shepheard's Hotel. Lots of men in linen suits with the women in straw hats and flowered cotton frocks. There was still polo and racing at the Gezira Club, dancing at the Auberge des Pyramides or Madam Badia's.

IBID, P.327

I remember Harry advising me in one of his more optimistic moments to bring my 'skunk' and silver fox, to combat the winter cold. And as for finding somewhere for us to live—he roped half of the women in Cairo into his search for a decent flat, had God knows how many near-misses (with accommodation, not the women) and grew increasingly mad about the whole thing. Then there was the 'small' matter of what we could actually afford; I even managed to claw £300 from Daddy so that Harry could buy furniture for one place he found. On top of all this, his (well, probably 'our') fussiness didn't help. He was doing his best to judge what we would both like and dislike (and what he thought he could let our illustrious friends actually see us living in). This led to many instant rejections; hell, he was obsessed with 'appearances'. And yes, that does make two of us … .

The other thing that drove us crazy was the post—well, the lack of it. While Harry probably wrote a few more letters than I did (almost ninety in eighteen months, in fact) we both endured long stretches of not knowing how the other was and not getting answers to the inevitable questions that we had for each other. Yes, we had been just as upset in South America but, as I think I said earlier, we *did* have a war to blame. Here we were casualties of a hopeless military balls up. On top of this they would change Harry's address at the drop of a hat just to add to our postal worries.

To keep me entertained Harry would lace his letters with filthy jokes and frequently remind me about how lonely 'Wilfred' was—this practice, of course, dated back to India, if not before, where he had some very earthy friends and by the end I was sending jokes back to him. One of his tamer offerings, no doubt triggered by local security rules went something like this: 'Fraternisation with locals is not permitted—copulation without conversation is *not* fraternisation!' Most were unrepeatable. By then I was giving him as good as I got …

All the same, Harry's optimism wasn't enough. We were

ground down by the cycle of optimism and despair and missed each other. Alasdair was away at Wellington in term time and I was lonely at Hove. Like-minded souls there were in short supply and I should have taken more notice of Harry's urgings to spend more time with Angela and Bunty. I hated the rationing—particularly of the food and clothes.

Talk about the boot being on the other foot: we had sent food and clothes parcels to the family in the early years of the war and now I relied on Harry's parcels from Cairo—rice, lard, cigarettes, dates, mangoes and endless supplies of Turkish delight. No surprise then that Harry's tales of being entertained with caviar, lobster and Champagne while on a trip to Turkey went down like a lead balloon.

> I've just got your letter, a very nice one darling, except that you still seem to want to keep a very strict eye on me! You just stop worrying your silly little head my sweetheart. I'm sorry to hear how bad your rations are getting now, the sooner I get you to Cairo the better—we will have a lovely time there. The food in this mess is very poor and is exactly what you would expect of a sergeant's mess. Ice is short so drinks are tepid and the national drinks like gin and cognac are by far the worst I have met. Quite good gin is available but here they seem to buy the most awful muck. For the past week we have had no lemon squash—every other mess has it. ... The most pleasant time here is in the evening when we congregate outside the mess for drinks at the outside bar. It is nice and cool there and with the lights on it looks much prettier than it actually is.
>
> HARRY TO ME, 29 JUNE 1945

He kept going:

> Darlingest Margaret ... This morning I got 3 letters from you, so I am now full of happiness, my beautiful one. ... It

looks as if the winter has started alright but that isn't at all bad really as there is usually plenty of sun. ... The material you have bought sounds lovely and I like the design you enclosed very much. When you come you will need both full evening dress and dinner dresses so you will have to decide what you're going to make this one up to. A full evening dress with the gold leather stuff sounds good to me. ... Max Fisher is arriving on Monday so I will remind him about the order for gin and whisky. Talking of liquor, I have a Fl/Lt in my section who really is on the verge of DTs. Funny what too much alcohol can do to one. I am damned surprised we got through South America so well considering what we consumed.

HARRY TO ME, 17 NOVEMBER 1945

And he did manage to spark some moments of light relief:

You will be pleased to hear that I went to Port Said on Wednesday night to meet Nick who had cabled me to say when he was arriving in *Royalist*. I managed to make it a duty visit so went in my car. I went on board about 7:00 pm and was most suitably entertained in the wardroom. We then had a gully-gully man on board who was very good.[4] I then told Nick that I had brought a girl from Cairo so he would have to dine with us ashore. That was alright but we first of all had to have a small session with the captain in his cabin. Eventually I got Nick off plus another commander and took them to the Casino Palace hotel where my 'girlfriend' was waiting.

---

[4] The gully-gully man was an Egyptian magician who visited ships that were moored up alongside the River Nile. He would entertain the crowd alongside other traders who sold souvenirs to the passengers on board, performing card, rope and coin tricks and his finale would be the 'cups and balls'.

> I introduced them and Nick made most polite conversation until 'girlfriend' couldn't stand it anymore and started laughing. Nick looked a bit mystified and then suddenly realised he had been making his polite conversation to his own cousin Rosemary! The other commander thoroughly enjoyed it as I had told him all about it beforehand. I don't know what Nick thought to himself before when I told him I had bought a girlfriend with me—he didn't tell me. Anyhow we had good fun that night and next day Rosemary and I had lunch on board with the captain.
>
> HARRY TO ME, 13 JANUARY 1946

At home, Mama's health got worse bit by bit, leading to a big panic in mid-'46. Daddy did his best to cope despite his age and even if we hadn't sold the car in readiness for my phantom trip to Egypt, I couldn't have got the petrol to drive over to Brighton as often as I should have done. At least they were no longer living at that huge house. Alasdair gave us a fright too, being rushed to hospital from school at some point for some reason that never became clear. It was something about 'late swelling' that was unusual in older boys and which foxed the doctors. After a spell of isolation in the school sanatorium he emerged as fit as a fiddle. I was worried.

No wonder I was smoking and drinking far too much. Alasdair didn't help by reminding me frequently that 40 or 50 cigarettes a day was not only bad for my health but an extremely expensive habit (and irritatingly providing the arithmetic to prove it.)

Thank Goodness Harry managed to wangle a couple of quick trips back to me. Otherwise I fear both of us would have suffered a complete melt-down. (I think that's what they call it these days.)

At some point Alasdair convinced himself that Harry had invented all the drama of his attempts to get me to Cairo and instead was having a field day with the women. Harry became 'the Father of Lies'—and would you believe, I couldn't persuade him that he had got it all wrong. Despite all Harry's revelations about his 'girlfriends' in his letters I trusted him more than I had ever done. His old insecurities had vanished— he knew I wasn't going to run away. And I was right. Sure, I was a mixture of upset and bored at his tales of endless cocktail parties, how it was just like the 'old days', meeting lots of our old pals who sent me their love and reminded him all the time 'how beautiful I was', etc. Well, he was there, blast it and I wasn't, even if Cairo was getting a bit sticky:

> We have been having lots of riots and we go about armed or are at times confined to our offices for the whole day. I expect you have read in the English papers how the mobs burnt and looted clubs, the cathedral etc. ...
>
> HARRY TO ME, 24 FEBRUARY 1946

Still, his sense of humour hung on. I was tickled pink that they described his team as 'Snow White and his seven dwarfs' as he had seven officers, most of them small; but somehow the 'Snow White' bit didn't quite fit. And then:

> Another story is—'a man asked a WAAC what the initials stood for and she said, "what about a cuddle?" He said 'by Jove, and to think that tomorrow I am going out with a WAAF'!
>
> HARRY TO ME, 2 MARCH 1946

Despite all this both he and I knew that we were stronger together and needed each other—and we weren't doing too badly—still lusting after each other after almost twenty years ... But 'Father of Lies' stuck; dear Angela kept it a family joke for years. And Alasdair, the (no-longer-little) monkey christened me 'Chow' but would never tell me why ...

Not long after the war ended Sylvia married Alan Davis. This time her engagement had stuck (I'd lost count of how many there had been). After a few months they shot off to Alan's hometown of Rochester in the USA. A well-established portrait painter and sculptress by then, she continued her work there and in New York with great success.

By the middle of 1946 we were at our wits' end. Car gone, baggage sent off to Cairo for my phantom trip, Air Ministry refusal to let me go, uncertainty over Harry's job (and future for that matter)—you name it, we had had enough…

> It looks very much as if you will not be able to come out officially—damn and blast the Air Force ruling. The only thing left therefore is to try and get out unofficially so get on to Pearson-Rogers to see if he can get you Air Ministry's permission to come out at your own expense. … I have just received your telegram saying Alasdair had some operation and was okay. This is the first I have heard about him needing one—I wonder what for, perhaps appendicitis. …
>
> Anyhow darling I'm determined to get you out here and, in the meantime, I am furious with the fatuous RAF. The army aren't going in for any of this nonsense and their wives are coming out OK. Would you start off making inquiries about boat passages? Altogether very depressed.
>
> HARRY TO ME, 13 MAY 1946

Bulgaria

Then out of the blue (in June), what did I think about going to Aden? By that time, I would have said 'yes' to almost anything … Yes, this really was 'fixed'—except of course it wasn't. After a month of shilly-shally, they decided to send him to Sofia instead, along with a promise that I could come too. Ho, Ho ... I had heard *that* before.

Nevertheless Harry was enthusiastic and believe it or not, off he went at the end of July. Just in time, really; anti-British demonstrations were increasing and Cairo was beginning to be a dangerous place. There were curfews and Harry had to carry a gun when outside. Alasdair looked on from the sidelines with some amusement. His letters around this time, even if sharpish at times, were long and entertaining.

> Dear Chow Reid, many thanks for your letter and the labels which all arrived this morning. Naturally Granny gets written to rather than you—she sends me parcels. If you do likewise, you may get a few more letters. Annoying about Father-of-Lies. I've just sent him some magazines to Aden. However, I expect he'll like Sofia as long as the Russians don't shoot him. Wouldn't it be awful if he'd been sent to Palestine?
>
> ALASDAIR TO ME, 23 JULY 1946

Although we didn't see it that way at the time, we did manage to inject some fun into the post-war muddle. Mother had some unbelievably valuable and magnificent jewellery—her 'rocks' as we called them. I had been allowed to wear some of them once or twice for super special occasions like our 1931 trip to the Palace. In '39 Daddy had the bright idea of sending them to me in Santiago (a) so that Hitler wouldn't get them and (b) for me to sell if everything blew up and we needed money. He seemed to forget that Harry adored seeing me wear them.

But then, what to do when we came back in '42? The U-boats were out in force and we didn't want the jewels to end up at the bottom of the Atlantic. So we locked them in one of the embassy safes, promising to get them out one day.

By the end of the war we were fed up with being strapped

for cash all the time; my allowances had just about vanished and Harry's income was never going to stretch to our rather extravagant way of life. Then, *voila*, there he was stuck in a city stuffed with endless numbers of people with more money than sense. So why not sell the jewels at a ridiculous price? Our worries would vanish. And so began 'Operation Rocks' …

Harry—never one to fight shy—wrote to the ambassador in Chile requesting that the jewels be sent to Cairo by diplomatic bag. Eventually this was done. They reached him just in time for the transfer to Aden that didn't happen. After much discussion (no time left to sell them) they found their way into the embassy safe in Cairo. Meanwhile we had kittens about the cost of insuring them (which got even worse when Harry moved on to Sofia.) Then followed endless debate about what to do with them—send them on to Sofia or back to England?

By this time, we had roped in half the diplomatic service trying to sort this out and the files were bursting with 'rocks' correspondence. In the end Harry took them on to Sofia.

His first reports of Bulgaria were mixed. He was there as part of the British Military Mission and had his hands full wrestling with Russians.[5]

Harry thought that Sofia was a dump. It crawled with the Red Army and had been fairly badly knocked about. He had

---

[5] 1944–47 was a tricky time for British political and military interests in the Balkans; much of it aimed at maintaining a buffer between Soviet domination in Russian-occupied countries and countries such as Greece and the wider Middle East and eastern Mediterranean. The Bulgaria Peace Treaty, which was eventually signed in Paris on 10 February 1947 and entered into force on 15 September 1947, required all the Allied Powers to withdraw their troops from Bulgaria within ninety days of that date. Overall, Soviet domination proved to be very oppressive and took the 'rights' enshrined in the Treaty with a pinch of salt.

Copy for
Group Captain
H. McLaren Reid.

No.40/62/46.

OFFICE OF THE BRITISH
POLITICAL REPRESENTATIVE
SOFIA

7th August, 1946.

(My dear Dunlop),

Here is a small problem which only requires one word from you to resolve.

Group Captain H. McLaren-Reid, who was formerly Air Attache at Santiago, having been transferred to Egypt and the United Kingdom, is now here. He left Chile in a hurry when the U-boats were rather active in 1942 and so he and his wife did not take her jewelry with them. When he got to Egypt where his wife was expected to join him he wrote to the Ambassador at Santiago and asked him to forward his wife's jewelry to him by bag. Leache did this and the jewelry turned up; but before his wife could join him, McLaren-Reid was transferred.

You will know how difficult the Egyptians are about refusing to let out of the country whatever has not been certified to have come into it - also how supine we British are in the face of such a ridiculous regulation by what ought to be a subject race. Anyway, the Group Captain brought the jewelry with him to Sofia from a R.A.F. (not Egyptian) aerodrome. And now, in view of the present uncertainty and the probable relatively short duration of the Military Mission's stay here, Mrs. McLaren-Reid is not going to join him; but she wants her jewelry.

May I, therefore, send under cover to you a small case containing this jewelry - none of which is liable to British Customs or purchase tax and which is insured item by item in London and so could easily be checked? If you will be good enough to let me send the package, perhaps you would then be so kind as to let Mrs. McLaren-Reid, who will be at Salisbury Lodge, Salisbury Road, Hove, Sussex, know that you have it and that you will hand it over to her if she will call at the Foreign Office to collect it.

(Thank you!
Yours ever,
(Sgd.) W. E. Houstoun-Boswall)

W. L. M. Dunlop, O.B.E.,
The Foreign Office,
S.W.1.

Letter from the 'Operation Rocks' correspondence, 7 August 1946.

however, been given a reasonable place to live—grand piano and all—and seemed to have done pretty well in training the staff.

Night life? Not a chance—no restaurants either. But he did discover plenty of entertainment in people's private houses, which really cheered him up. The British girls at the Legation and Mission on the other hand were thoroughly fed up as the boys ignored them in favour of local lasses (apparently very easy on the eye) whom they brought along to these parties.

At last I was called for—hoorah! Harry had got a clear steer over his future and was expected to stay on until the peace treaty that they were all heading towards had been ratified.

After the Air Ministry's complete failure—refusal, actually—to get me out to Cairo, you can imagine my surprise when out of the blue, at the end of September, I got what amounted to an instruction to hurry off to Northolt Airport where a Wellington bomber was waiting to whisk me off to Sofia. Yes, I knew how ill Mama was and how my exit would upset Daddy but I was past caring. I packed a suitcase, phoned a quick goodbye to Alasdair and off I went ... .

Irony of ironies, when I reached Sofia, the 'rocks' were on their way back to London. Immaterial when compared to our joy at being together again: to all intents and purposes we had been apart for the best part of a year and a half. I know this must sound like small beer compared with the aching separations so many had suffered during the war, but even so ... .

Do you know? It wasn't bad—not quite the 'cesspit' that Daddy called it. There were disturbances and the place bristled with guns. Harry and I just got on with life once more; it was just marvellous to be together again. I managed to jolly up our villa and to muster some friends. While Harry didn't get any local allowances, everything (and I mean everything) was provided—house, servants, food, booze and transport in the shape of a Buick that rattled; the lot. We even developed a taste for slivovitz—needed it to keep warm that winter and weeks below zero [Fahrenheit]. The post wasn't bad, so we had plenty of news from home. We even managed to telephone Alasdair on his birthday. He was so excited.

> It was great fun being rung up by you the other day. A wonderful surprise when we were told to stand by for a call from Bulgaria. ... Many thanks indeed for the chess set, which is going to be very useful at college, sitting in its box the way it does. I am going up to see 'Worms Eye View' at the Whitehall on Saturday, as a birthday present from Aunty Angela. A very nice one. You're paying for my lunch [at Claridge's], journey etc. via the £1/- which you gave me on the telephone.
> ALASDAIR TO 'CHOW AND FATHER OF LIES', 9 JANUARY 1947

Letters from home also kept us well informed of Mama's steady decline and Daddy didn't expect her to last long. She died in January, having been ill for a long time and pretty much bedridden. Angela, bless her, spent most of her daytimes caring for her. Alasdair was with her too.

She had a good send off, but as Nick and I were both away, it fell to Angela and Alasdair to look after him at her funeral. They buried her at Hove.

A few weeks later Daddy was scared stiff by the reports of the 'disturbance' of 7 March when Bulgarian thugs surrounded Harry's office, our house and all the other diplomatic places as part of a phony complaint about currency fiddles. They were bloody rude. Harry—at least six inches taller than any of them—had plenty to say to them and terrified them. At the same time, we heard of growing violence between Muslims and bands of Hindus and Sikhs in and around Rawalpindi, as India veered towards partition. We were really upset about this: we had been there just ten years before and had fond memories of all these people.

On the plus side, Alasdair kept us entertained with long

letters full of advice about what car we should buy (very well researched I might add) and how to minimise related taxes. His antics on various motorcycles and a blow-by-blow account of an accident and its fallout, however, terrified me—wasn't he rather young to be dicing with the law? He delighted in reporting that his cousin Martin referred to Harry as 'a dirty Bulgarian' and that 'by the way, it is definitely time that you got me a dinner jacket'.

Earlier on he had remained remarkably calm about his army selection process, with in-depth accounts of his medical and the Regular Commissions Board. And to think that a muddle about his name was the only time he sounded rattled.

> I told you in my last letter how the army examiners wanted a photograph. Yesterday they sent an inquiry about my names. (They'd wanted the birth certificate). They wanted to know why it was Alasdair Harry McLaren Reid when I wrote it myself and Harry Alastair McLaren Reid on my certificate. You've certainly let your poor son in for a lot of trouble with the ridiculous muddle you made when I was born. The army examiners also sent a special form to be filled up asking 'are you unmarried?'
>
> ALASDAIR TO 'CHOW, FATHER AND OTHERS', 19 OCTOBER 1946

As his last days at Wellington loomed, we heard that he had got into Sandhurst. His last report concluded:

> His development has been slow for his years, but satisfactory and he may well go far as a soldier. He has been a Dormitory Prefect for the last two weeks and I have found him most helpful and conscientious.
>
> WELLINGTON COLLEGE, LENT TERM, 1947

So that was it: Alasdair began army training, which of course finally put a stopper on his elaborate plans to visit us in

Sofia. Beginning with a spell at Caterham, they sent him to Ireland where he spent an arduous summer in readiness for Sandhurst in the autumn. Harry made all sorts of effort to help him get into the Irish Guards which, unsurprisingly, were all in vain as Alasdair was a Scot. He was rather miffed.

By the time we left Sofia late in 1947 I had been there for well over a year. Despite the local tensions, we had had some fun, enjoyed the countryside and eventually made some good Bulgarian friends; the mountains had lots of charm and we found pleasant spots on the Black Sea coast. We even managed to wangle some leave in Vienna.

Within a year Harry would be out of uniform and I would have lasted twenty-one years as an RAF wife. Just think—eleven houses, heaven knows how many miles and far too much alcohol. Thick and thin in almost equal measure? Probably!

Would Harry cope? Or indeed, would I?

Chapter 17
Fading away

> There are plenty of American nylons here
> [in Germany] so I can send you some if you let me
> know all the details such as deniers, size, colour etc.
> The shops are full of everything like that you
> cannot see in England.
> ALASDAIR TO ME, 9 SEPTEMBER 1951

Harry retired in February 1948. His 30 years were up and civvy street finally caught up with the two of us. He was 48. We found a place in Chelsea and thankfully, unlike some of our friends, we could manage to wash a cup and saucer without endless complaint about the lack of servants. We were happy to be free.

And guess what was one of the first things he did? You remember he had pretended to be 'McLaren-Reid' rather than plain 'Reid' ever since I'd known him: well, he set about formalising this by deed poll and so by the end of the year it was official—not just for him but also Alasdair and me. Well!

All the while Alasdair was bedding in happily at Sandhurst; even though he hadn't managed to get into a posh infantry regiment (settling for the gunners) he sounded fine (*see overleaf*).

Daddy died in '49. The Brighton folk flocked to his funeral and the lavish wake that followed and—*en passant*—the local rag lost one of its more colourful contributors.

As for Harry's siblings, Toby had returned to his customs work at Kuala Lumpur and Sylvia flourished in the USA, where she was establishing herself at the Rochester Institute of

Technology teaching painting and fine arts. We did our best to keep in touch, but they both grew increasingly far away. We missed them.

Harry had several jobs which I won't pretend he enjoyed. He even had a spell with a driving school. At some point however I had the bright idea of investing my inheritance in London property, when you could pick up a decent place for

Alasdair as a dashing new subaltern in the Royal Artillery, 1948.

well under £2,000—less, if one of the thousands damaged during the war. You know, it worked. Harry did much of the 'hunting and selling' and arguing with builders and the like. It helped too that he could make things—do anything with his hands. His knowledge, eye for detail and persistence endlessly frustrated the builders, but they did listen to him. As for me, I designed the interiors. Style has always mattered to me and I had a flair for this—all that work sorting out homes over the years suddenly put to use. New textiles and colours were beginning to appear to brighten up the post-war gloom. I loved it. We made a packet.

There was a moment when he found an old Bristol Fighter that he wanted to restore—he longed to pull it to pieces and bring it back to life and hoped he could interest some of his old No. 6 Squadron pals in the project. But all this faded away when matching enthusiasm and funding failed to appear ... Shame.

London was a real muddle in the early '50s—bombed out buildings waiting to be cleared, rationing, smog, poverty and the occasional scandal ... Delights were pretty scarce, but we did get to Henley and a garden party at the Palace in '52, which were nice run-ups to our silver wedding celebrations a few months later.

Alasdair kept us nicely up to date. He joined a gunner unit in Germany in the early fifties and seemed to flourish there— made friends, travelled far and wide and managed to keep himself well entertained—catching up with us on his occasional trips to England. He wrote long letters and gave us a blow-by-blow account of an epic 4,000-mile drive to Jordan en route to the Suez Canal Zone with a fellow officer in '54.[6]

---

[6] After the Second World War British soldiers garrisoned bases on the Suez Canal in Egypt to maintain control of the canal. Between 1950 and 1954 they were subjected to regular attacks by local nationalists, including a general revolt at Ismailia in 1952.

His car made it all the way and just managed to get over a couple of high passes in Austria—apparently it didn't like Austrian petrol. He ended up in a tented camp near Fayid on the shores of the Great Bitter Lake—it's part of the Suez Canal and both Harry and I had sailed through it on our various voyages. By the time Alasdair got there, the zone had been under regular attack by Egyptian nationalists for some time and around 50 British servicemen had been killed: it wasn't that safe a place to be. Security was tight. I fretted while Harry—very impressed by Alasdair's long journey—saw it all as par for the course …

Around this time we moved to a rather lovely house in Princes Gate Mews in South Kensington. But old cobbled streets, proximity to Hyde Park and other delights were not enough to alter the fact that Harry found civilian life tedious. The old hunter gave up work in 1959 and we left London for good. Still, we had managed to find some excitement—kept up with friends, entertained as much as we could, managed to keep our wardrobes and dancing skills intact and listened to heaps of jazz in seedy nightclubs: shame that we left just weeks before Ronnie Scott opened up in Frith Street—that *would* have been fun.

We set ourselves up in Sussex to be close to friends and relations. Angela and Maurice had moved to Haywards Heath, which meant that we saw a lot of each other. Sadly, we invariably drank too much and Harry and Maurice would end up arguing; drove me and Angela mad—they never seemed to learn.

Then in 1965 I sold my share of Mama's diamonds and we bought the Old Mill House at Coombe Bissett near Salisbury. We had a rather wider circle of friends and acquaintances there which—naturally—I continued to cultivate. The village suited us right down to the ground. The place was stiff with old soldiers and airmen who had grown up on and around the Plain and seemed unable to stay away; Harry had been stationed around here goodness knows how many times—no shortage of generals either.

The house—a wonderful Georgian pile complete with ancient wooden barn and paddock—is lovely (*see overleaf*). Plenty of character and more than enough space for all the furniture, rugs and other bits and pieces we accumulated from our travels. And the garden ... perfect for summer parties and bursting with hideaways for those who wanted to misbehave. Harry was in fishing heaven—the River Ebble, a sleepy chalk stream, flowed alongside the house and he was within spitting distance of some of the best waters for brown trout in England. There were salmon too.

And for the first time in our married life we weren't short of cash ... Harry bought a Rolls and careered around the place even though the thing barely fitted into all the narrow roads around us. Miracle that he didn't hit anything (or anyone).

The village itself was small, most of it strung out along a spider's web of small roads leading from the Salisbury-Blandford highway. It had all we needed—shop, school, village hall, pub and a thriving cricket club.

Just to add to the merry-go-round, we found that Bonzo was farming at Farley—a village ten miles or so away on the opposite side of Salisbury, not far from his old gunner stomping grounds at Larkhill. After India he had a 'good' war in spite of a short stint as a PoW in 1944 and was by now a local big shot—high sheriff and all that—and, same as ever, hadn't let this go to his head. His wife was delightful. We saw him from time to time and, to Angela's unending irritation, enjoyed his company once more; as far as she was concerned, he was still a very naughty boy.

Talking of Angela, Maurice was knighted in 1961 so she is now Lady Whittome. Nick's knighthood was announced on the very same day—he had reached the dizzy heights of Vice-Admiral after a string of top naval appointments. How about that? (Harry was just a tiny bit envious, grumbling in his off

The Old Mill House at Coombe Bissett, 2021.

moments at the number of his old colleagues who had risen high in the RAF. Robert Saundby, who had been his CO at Aden, was now an Air Marshall).

Toby died just before we left London. He had worked as an administrator on Christmas Island for several years and had just retired to live in Sussex. He and Bunny had just returned for UK leave when he suffered a severe stroke at the end of 1958. Despite his bravado he never really recovered from his treatment by the Japanese—such a far, far cry from our rather cushy war. No children. No new Reids …

Sylvia did her best to keep in touch. Among other things she was a founder-member of a group of artists from Rochester in New York State who called themselves the 'Arena Group'. We have some of her paintings. Her husband Alan died early in the '70s and she now soldiers on alone. I read a lovely quote from Sylvia somewhere during the '50s. An artist to the core, it went something like this:

The American doesn't seem interested in the intrinsic merit of a work of art, a house, an automobile, a horse, a dog. The price of the article or animal is what is emphasised. It is a little disconcerting at first; though of course you become in time used to it.

The fact was that so many loved ones and friends were dying. Brother Nick went in 1969, followed by Bunty a few years later and Angela has just lost Maurice. Harry's mother kept going to the ripe old age of ninety-five, when she died—still compos mentis—at a home in Surrey. Harry was always very loyal to her and—helped by Sylvia and Toby—had covered for her financially for ages.

But there was still our son. Sadly as far as Harry was concerned, Alasdair was a disappointment. He was not married and showed no signs of doing so. No wife meant no heir: no more McLaren-Reids. He had made it through Sandhurst and as far as we could tell was doing well as a gunner—stints in Germany and the Canal Zone in the early 1950s—and was a major by the time he was thirty-four: very respectable.

We gave up hoping he might marry and give us some grandchildren. Along the way I introduced him to some delightful young ladies but he would not bite—I often wonder where we went wrong ... I mean, it must have been our fault *somehow*.

But then he resigned from the Army just after we had left for Wiltshire and he retreated to our old flat in Chelsea. We never knew why. There was gossip about an 'incident' with a fellow officer which turned out to be twaddle.

Whatever happened, he just seemed to lose his way. It was as if he saw himself as a great failure. We couldn't make it out and he wouldn't talk to us. He just drifted further and further from us despite my efforts. I tried to get him to talk to a therapist but got nowhere. What was buried in his head that troubled him so? Were we to blame?

It's getting late. I'm beginning to feel cold and know that I'm running out of steam. Harry has been wonderful—there's nothing he won't do for me. We've been married for over 50 years and I still love him to bits.

Wilfred is now hors de combat—has been for a few years now (no damage—just old age), but what a record ... Apropos of Wilfred, while Horace was perfectly competent, Harry was a maestro: even today he purrs when I remind him of this. We still cuddle each other ... .

I'll stop now and turn off the machine. Don't you think we had a good run? You know, I kept all those letters. I wonder if anyone will read them ... .

> I, ALASDAIR HARRY McLAREN-REID, of 6, Eaton Mews North, in the city of Westminster, an Officer Cadet of The Royal Military Academy, Sandhurst, a natural born British subject, hereby give notice that I have assumed for myself and for any children and remoter issue I may have, and intend henceforth upon all occasions and at all times to sign and use and be called and known by the surname of McLaren in addition to my present surname of Reid and as a hyphenated prefix thereto and so that my new surname and that of my family as aforesaid shall henceforth be McLaren-Reid. And further I hereby give notice (a) that I have absolutely renounced and abandoned the use of my former Christian name of Alastair (as registered at my birth), and have adopted in lieu thereof the Christian name of Alasdair; and (b) that I have absolutely renounced and abandoned the use of my former Christian name of McLaren and so that my full names shall now read only as follows:— Alasdair Harry McLaren-Reid, and that such intended change or assumption of name is formally declared and evidenced by a deed poll under my hand and seal dated the 1st day of October, 1948, and enrolled in the Central Office of the Supreme Court of Judicature on the 12th day of October, 1948.
>
> In testimony whereof I hereby sign and subscribe myself by such my intended future name.—Dated this 19th day of October, 1948.
> (191) ALASDAIR HARRY McLAREN-REID.

Chapter 18
Aftermath—as reported

> He was born in Scotland but his parents lived in
> Argentina. And then they left Argentina and they just
> left everything behind, they left the whole farm—it's
> still there. He was brought up gaucho style; then he
> was sent back to England to be educated. And he met
> my great aunt in Iraq.
>
> CATRIONA NEWINGTON, MARGARET'S GREAT NIECE, APRIL 2003

And now it is time for your humble author to take over and tidy up. Let me start by saying that Margaret 'Chow' McLaren-Reid—she of the cocktail voice—died on 29 December 1979. She had been ill for a while and suffered a massive stroke. Her husband Harry, 'Father-of-Lies', who cared for her with such love, rather fell apart once she had gone. Nothing that the doting ladies in the village did to console him worked. His eyesight deteriorated and he found it increasingly difficult to fend for himself. He died just before Christmas 1986 in Odstock hospital at Salisbury, where he had spent the last six weeks of his life. To his joy, his widowed sister Sylvia crossed the Atlantic and managed to reach him just before he went into hospital. He was eighty-seven. It was a sad year for the wider family too—Angela had died six months earlier.

After the Army, Alasdair set himself up in London and got a job buying, selling and renting cars. No one was surprised—he knew the difference between a big end and a tappet way before his contemporaries could do long-division. By the time he was ten he was giving his parents considered advice on what car to buy and he had a particular yen for style which, when mixed with big horsepower, tended to point to some very expensive motors. He had driven half-way round Europe not to mention his trip to the Middle East: as far as cars were concerned, he knew his stuff.

He lived way beyond his means and entertained lavishly—took half the ladies in London out to lovely restaurants, it is said. Habitually short of money, he shifted to a dismal bedsit to which no one was ever invited and which didn't even have a bathroom. He and alcohol became close friends.

Regardless of the love-hate relationship with his parents, Alasdair travelled down to them most weekends and kept a watchful eye over Harry after Margaret's death.

Despite their differences father and son still cared for each other. When he died Harry left Alasdair a small fortune and a large-enough cheque to enable him to pay the inevitable death duties. The son and heir was suddenly rather comfortably off and—true to form—managed to burn a lot of money over the years that followed.

Right on cue, a large car dealership in Salisbury offered him a job. He moved into the Old Mill House, became well known in the village and remained there for the rest of his life. His existence at the house was spartan—rattling around in the few rooms that he used and doing nothing to the overall building fabric.

He did his best to keep the Fox and Goose [his local] in profit. He would often stagger across the road and paddle across the Ebble to take a short cut home after a heavy night.

Sylvia died in New York late in the 1980s. Alasdair, who had kept in touch with her, had hoped that some of her estate might come his way as she had no children. In the event, and to Alasdair's inevitable chagrin, she donated all her money to arts foundations in the USA.

After the storm of January 1990 took away the great barn at the Old Mill House, Alasdair sought advice about the resilience of the house itself. Advised to reinforce the roof space, particularly the joists and predictably reluctant to pay for the cost of work, he came up with a rather simple but radical solution: much better to remove the load on the upstairs ceiling all together. Into a skip went the whole contents of the loft: countless fur coats, all his father's and grandfather's fishing rods and associated tackle, unused artefacts, enough books to fill a library and heaven knows what else. Problem solved.

How would he have regarded his parents? I suspect that underneath it all he would have remembered his mother as a bright, beautiful and generous soul who really struggled with her loyalties, particularly between him and Harry; but foxy, too. 'That' photograph still has pride of place in the various family homes.

He might have been less charitable about Harry. True, he was a fine and brave airman who somehow managed to avoid that 'one prang too many': tough and macho to the end. But his overbearing presence and monotonous disappointment at the lack of grandchildren was hard to take. Still, he would not have denied that the old bugger had style—they both did. Perhaps not so strangely, the 'old soldier' in him did recognise the contributions that both his father and uncle Toby had made to their country: he thought they should be remembered and so passed on their medals, Harry's flying log books and Toby's experiences as a Japanese PoW to the Imperial War Museum, where they can be seen today.

Then, there was always a lingering doubt that he just couldn't match their expectations, especially his perception that he turned out to be a poor substitute for David (hypothetically, how would *he* have coped with being dumped with his grandparents for years)?

But in his heart of hearts he suspected that, while they never admitted it, they blamed themselves for the 'mess' that *they* thought he became.

It was Alasdair who found the tapes. He came across them while sorting out Harry's junk and hired someone to transcribe them. Someone else did a quick edit. He was surprised. Margaret's story revealed obvious affection for him and his safety and the revelations proved to be a great healer, helping a process that grew over the years that followed, soothing his long-term depression.

This is the firm belief of Angela's successors, some of whom still live in her final home. Between them they have fond memories of this big, larger-than-life, funny and generous man. They are convinced that Alasdair began to understand and forgive his parents, and to realise that he was a victim of the times rather than of simple selfish neglect. Service families had to move around. It was normal to send their children away, not only because of the perception that it was 'character-building' but because it brought an otherwise impossible continuity to their schooling. And he did love India, where they had had time to be a proper family. It was the war that came along and messed everything up.

And how should *we* see Harry and Margaret now? Through today's lens they might seem a little murky, but in hindsight that might not be so fair.

> Margaret met her first husband at a convalescent home in Wales … Harry would have been very jealous of anyone getting anyone near Margaret … Harry was with some very dishy girls on the way; in those days it was alright for a man to have other women, but vice versa 'no'.
>
> MARTIN WHITTOME, APRIL 2003

Angela's daughter-in-law remembers Harry and Margaret with affection. She recalls a lovely, funny and charming man who was in his element at gatherings—surrounded by young people who adored him—'a magnet'. She has a rather delightful anecdote about Harry. Alarmed both by Harry's growing blindness and his insistence on driving, Alasdair arranged for someone to visit from Salisbury to test his vision. A lady optician travelled to Coombe Bisset by bus and, as anticipated, she certified Harry's eyesight as not far short of blind. Ever the gentleman, Harry offered to give her a lift home. Horrified, she gently declined his offer and headed for the bus stop. Not long afterwards Harry bowed to the inevitable and sold the Rolls.

But there were a few chinks in his armour—maybe some underlying insecurities or a slight inferiority complex—not quite from the right stock, perhaps?

While he was so proud to be a Scot, he never let it creep into his speech. He has been described as an utter snob, thinking plain 'Reid' was common as muck. And as we have seen, his early obsession with the double-barrelled name assumed when young led him to formalise it after the war. And behind the upper class swagger he was something of a bully, determined to get his own way and not one to oppose. (Maurice is said to have thought he was 'thick as shit', but that might have had more to do with an Old Etonian deriding an Old Harrovian). I'm not sure how he would have coped with political correctness but maybe that's a red herring.

And Margaret? She was born into a privileged world that, although rocked by the First World War, still retained conventions that she was brave enough to challenge. Yes, she did allow herself to be swept up by the speed and glamour of the '20s and all that went with it but did go on to adapt to life brilliantly in different and challenging environments. Posh? Well, they were and behaved as posh people did then. Margaret deserves to be remembered as more than just someone who wore beautiful clothes and lived in endless pursuit of fun. And without question, she and Harry were devoted to each other.

Alasdair died in July 2011. The church at his funeral was packed. He left The Old Mill House plus the contents to

Angela's granddaughter, Catriona—his goddaughter. She remembers Alasdair with great affection and still has furniture and other artefacts that Harry and her Great Aunt brought back from afar, along with enough silver to feed a regiment; they look just as good today as ever.

While she was closing up the house she made a final visit to the pub. Seeking some closure about the rumours about Alasdair's sexuality she asked one of the women behind the bar at The Fox and Goose if she thought he was gay. She grinned knowingly and said with some confidence that he was not. I think we will leave it there.

Fin de ligne indeed …

THE END

Appendix
Harry Reid's Service Record: 1918–1948

From RAF Pilot to Military Liaison Officer

Date	Station	Rank	Function/ Position
10.03.18	Greenwich	Temp.Prob. Flight Officer	
01.04.18		Flying Officer RAF	
26.05.18	Uxbridge		Armament School
01.06.18	Stamford		HQ 35th Wing
24.08.18		2nd Lt 'A' RAF	
25.09.18			No. 5 Training Depot Station
06.01.19	Wittering		No. 1 Training Depot Station (Asst. Instr.)
08.02.19			No. 5 Training Depot Station
12.03.19			To Unemployment list
16.04.21			No. 1 Group HQ (Temporary Duty)
05.06.21			To Unemployment list
05.07.21		Flying Officer	School of Technical Training (Flying refresher)

AIRCRAFT FLOWN

AIRCRAFT	ENGINE	AIRCRAFT	ENGINE	AIRCRAFT	ENGINE
		HAWKER INTERCEPTOR			
D.H.6		ATLAS.		FURY.	
B.E. 2 C.		ATLAS MK II.		TUTOR.	
" 2 D.		FOKKER.		HART.	
" 2 E.		III F.		BRISTOL 120.R.b.	
AVRO	LE RHONE.	STARLING.		WESTLAND P.G.	
"	CLERGET.	BULLDOG.		AUDAX.	
"	MONO.	VENTURE.		SEAL.	
"	LYNX.	BRISTOL 109.		TOMTIT.	
R.E.8M.		FLEETWING.		VILDEBEESTE.	
BRISTOL FIGHTER	ARAB.	HORNET.		WALLACE.	
" "	ROLLS.	HINAIDI.		R.2.	
" "	RAPIER.	RIPON.		WHITNEY STRAIGHT.	
A.W. (SMALL)		HYENA.		MAGISTER.	
A.W. 10		SIDESTRAND.		MONOSPAR.	
HIPPO.		WAPITI.		MILES HAWK.	
D.H.9A.	LIBERTY.	HORSLEY.		OXFORD	
"	LION.	HAWKER F.20/27		WACO.	
SISKIN.		WESSEX.		PROCTOR.	
NIGHT HAWK.		FLYCATCHER.			
DART.		BLOODHOUND.			
VIRGINIA.		AJAX.			
MOTH.		GORDON.			
PUSS MOTH.		FOX.			
HYDERABAD		NIMROD.			

Harry's logbook recording the various classes of aircraft he had flown.

31.01.22	No. 6 Sqn.		**Iraq** (Flying)
12.02.23		Flying Officer (Perm.)	
27.12.24	No. 208 Sqn.		**Middle East** (Flying)
24.06.25	Aden		**Middle East** (Flying)
31.12.25			RAF Inland Area (UK Leave)
01.02.25	Cranwell		Flying
03.06.26			Flying Instructor refreshed course
19.07.26	No.5 FTS		Flying Instructor
12.10.26	Cranwell		Flying Instructor
01.07.27		Flight Lieutenant	
17.07.29	Farnborough		Training as Experimental and Test Pilot
19.11.29	Farnborough		Experimental and Test Pilot
01.03.32			Sick
12.05.32	No. 22 Sqn.		Bomber: experimental duties
04.09.32			School of Army Co-operation course
26.11.32	No. 22 Sqn.		Bomber: experimental duties
07.02.33	No. 5 Sqn.		**India** (Flying)
21.11.34	No. 20 Sqn.		**India** (Flying)
30.09.35	No. 20 Sqn.		**India** (Admin)
01.02.36		Squadron Leader	
25.02.36	No. 5 Sqn.		To command
18.04.37			UK Leave
08.08.37	Odiham		Air staff duties
12.07.38			**South America** Assistant Air Attaché
01.01.39		Wing Commander	

01.06.41		Group Captain	**South America** Air Attaché
1942	Farnborough		
1945	Caserta, Italy		Foreign Liaison, **Italy**
1945	Cairo		Foreign Liaison, **Egypt**
1946-8	Sofia		British Military Mission, **Bulgaria**
1948			Retired

[Reproduced from formal RAF Officers' Records, as recorded on 5 April 1938, and with numerous subsequent handwritten updates. These would routinely include any related items of distinction, such as the 'Honours and Mentions' and 'Special Qualifications' quoted below.]

Honours and Mentions

- DFC Kurdistan L.G., 11.06.24

- 'Brought to notice by GOC Aden Command for skill and keenness during operation in the hinterland of Aden during four months ending 09.11.25.'

- 'Awarded special notation in recognition of distinguished service in Iraq Sept. November 1924.'

Special Qualifications

- Flying Instructor Cat. A.2; Adverse reports: Nil.

Acknowledgements

This book would probably have remained unwritten had it not been for Cat Newington's wholehearted support. She is both Margaret's great-niece and Alasdair's goddaughter and not only gave me free access to Margaret's photo albums and a mountain of family ephemera but also introduced me to her parents, Martin and Margaret and her uncle Giles, all of whom knew the McLaren-Reids and of their lives.

The book would have been very different had it not been for the advice (or perhaps insistence) of my writing friends in Oxford—Andrew Bartholomew, Robert Bullard, Pauline Cakebread, Ian Hembrow and Nigel Moor—who urged me to write the story from Margaret's point of view rather than Harry's (as I had planned).

Others to whom I am indebted include: Moniek van de Ven, who helped me through the whole process, including transcribing some of the letters; Margery Pearl Gurnet, who found me details of Sylvia Davis's life in the USA; Graham Pitchfork, who kindly wrote the Foreword and explained the role of air attachés; Joanna Badrock, the archivist at Harrow School; Caroline Jones, the archivist at Wellington College; Henry Meadows, the auctioneer who put me in touch with Cat; and the Collections Enquiry team at the RAF Museum, Hendon.

I am grateful to the Imperial War Museum for access to the Private Papers of Group Captain H.R. McLaren-Reid, with the comment that 'Every effort has been made to trace copyright holders and the Author and the Imperial War Museum would be grateful for any information which might help to trace those whose identities or addresses are not currently known.'

Finally, it would be very remiss of me not to thank Stephen Games, my editor, not only for his meticulous scrutiny of the text and attention to detail but also for his many suggestions that have added necessary clarity (not forgetting solving some of the thornier difficulties involved with those departures from Margaret's voice). The book is richer for his determination, insight and design.

Abbreviations

ADC	Aide-de-camp
AFALS	Allied Forces Air Liaison Service
AMC	Alfred Heathcote Copeman
AOC	Air Officer Commanding
APO	Assistant Political Officer
AVM	Air Vice Marshall
BA	Buenos Aires
BF	Bristol Fighter
CMG	Companion of the Order of St Michael and St George
CO	Commanding Officer
DFC	Distinguished Flying Cross
DTs	*delirium tremens* (severe alcohol withdrawal)
DSO	Distinguished Service Order
FTS	Flying Training School
HMG	His Majesty's Government
IA	Indian Army
KCMG	Knight Commander of the Order of St Michael and St George
LG	London Gazette
NAAFI	Navy, Army and Air Force Institutes
NCO	Non-commissioned Officer
NWF	North West Frontier
PA	Personal Assistant
PoW	Prisoner of war
RAF	Royal Air Force

SHAEF	Supreme Headquarters, Allied Expeditionary Force
SASO	Senior Air Staff Officer
UK	United Kingdom
VE	Victory in Europe
VJ	Victory over Japan
WAAC	Women's Auxiliary Army Corps (USA)
WAAF	Women's Auxiliary Air Force (UK)

Bibliography

PUBLICATIONS

Atchinson, K., *Unknown Brighton*, Bodley Head, 1926.

Cooper, Artemis, *Cairo in the war 1939-1945*, Hamish Hamilton, London 1989.

Edmonds C.J., *Kurds, Turks and Arabs*, OUP, 1957.

Fieldhouse D.K. (ed), *Kurds, Arabs and Britons: The Memoir of Lieutenant-Colonel W.A. Lyon CBE in Iraq 1918–44*, I.B. Tauris, 2001.

Greig, D'Arcy, Ed. Franks, N. and Muggleton, S., *My Golden Flying Years: From 1918 Over France, Through Iraq in the 1920s, to the Schneider Trophy Race of 1929*, Grub Street, London 2010.

Hayward J., Birch D., Bishop R., *British Battles and Medals*, 7th Ed., Spink, 2006, p. 517

IWM Documents.232, Private Papers of Group Captain H.R. McLaren-Reid D.F.C., Entries in pilot's log books.

Kennedy, H., Khadduri, M. et al, 'Iraq', Encyclopaedia Britannica, Inc., (8 October 2020), https://www.britannica.com/place/Iraq. Accessed 13 October 2020.

London Gazette, AVM Salmond's despatch of 11 June 1923.

Mackrell, J., *Flappers: Six Women of a Dangerous Generation*, Pan Macmillan, 2013.

Noel, Edward, 'The Character of the Kurds as Illustrated by Their Proverbs and Popular Sayings', *Bulletin of the School of Oriental Studies*, University of London, Vol. 1, No. 4 (1920), pp. 79–90.

Omissi, David, *Indian Voices of the Great War: Soldiers' Letters 1914–18*, MacMillan, 1999.

Philpot, Ian M., 'The Royal Air Force 1930–1939', *An Encyclopaedia of the Inter-War Years, 1939-1939*, Pen and Sword, 2008.

Renfrew, Barry. *'Wings of Empire': The Forgotten Wars of the Royal Air Force, 1919–1939*, The History Press, 2018.

Royal Air Force Historical Branch, *The RAF: Small Wars and Insurgencies in the Middle East, 1919–1939*, (2011) pp 7–20.

Shrimpton, Jayne, *Fashion in the 1920s*, Shire Publications, 2013.

Satia, Priya, 'The Defense of Inhumanity: Air Control and the British Idea of Arabia', *The American Historical Review*, Volume 111, Issue 1, February 2006.

Somerrell, D.C., *A History of Tonbridge School*, Faber & Faber, 1947.

Stankova, Marietta. *Bulgaria in British Foreign Policy, 1943–49*, LSE PhD thesis, 1939, various.

The National Archives:
AIR 2 'Recommendations for awards'.
AIR 27/63/15 No. 15 Squadron: Operations Record Book.
AIR 27/258/3 No. 20 Squadron: Operations Record Book 1933-35.

Venn, John, *Alumni Cantabrigienses: A Biographical List of All Known Students, Graduates and Holders of Office at the University of Cambridge, from the Earliest Times to 1900*, Vol. 1, CUP 1922.

INTERNET

140th Field Regiment (5th London) Field Regiment, Royal Artillery, Biography of Lt Col Cedric Odling, *http://140th-field-regiment-ra-1940.co.uk/biographies/lt-col-cedric-odling*. Accessed 5 Feb 2022.

Arena Art Group, *https://www.arenaartgroup.org/read-me*. Accessed 21 May 2021

British Geriatric Society, As we once were; Wartime rationing, *https://www.bgs.org.uk/resources/as-we-once-were-wartime-rationing*, Michael Denham, November 2014, accessed 3 Aug 2022

Campaign Summaries Of World War 2, German U-Boats At War, Part 1 of 6, 1939–40, *https://www.naval-history.net/WW2 CampaignsUboats.htm*. Accessed 12 Mar 2021

Christmas Island, *https://www.worldstatesmen.org/Christmas_Island.html*. Accessed 10 Feb 2024

Early Kurdish nationalism, *https://en.wikipedia.org/wiki/Early_Kurdish_nationalism*, accessed 13 Jul 2022

Junkers JU-90, https://en.wikipedia.org/wiki/Junkers_Ju_90, accessed 17 May 2021

Lawrence, C.A., 'Iraq Revolt of 1920' (Jan 2016), Dupuy Institute, *http://www.dupuyinstiute.org/blog/2016/01/11/iraq-revolt-of-1920/*, accessed 13 Oct 2020

Online resources*: https://www.ancestry.co.uk/, https://d-maps.com, https://www.findmypast.co.uk/*

Royal Air Force Airpower Review, (2002) 'Templar Lecture 2001', *https://www.raf.mod.uk/what-we-do/centre-for-air-and-space-power-studies/documents1/air-power-review-vol-4-no-2/*, accessed 15 Oct 2020

Rules restaurant during the war, *https://rules.co.uk/restaurant/history/*, accessed 8 Feb 2024

Doctor Brighton's Pavilion, *https://www.sikhmuseum.com/brighton/*, accessed 17 Jan 2024

Six Squadron Association, *https://sixsqnassociation.org.uk/about/1919-1935/*, accessed 29 Oct 2021

Suez Canal Zone crisis, *https://www.militaryhistoryonline.com/Modern/EgyptCanalGuerrillas*, accessed 11 Feb 2024

NEWSPAPERS
Cheltenham Chronicle, 7 June 1924.
Western Daily Herald, 1 June 1924.

Quotations and Illustrations

Most quotations in the book are taken from letters to Margaret McLaren-Reid in the author's collection.

The few short quotations come either from books that are acknowledged individually or from conversations with the Whittome and Newington families, to whom I am indebted.

All images are the author's reproductions of photographs and family ephemera belonging to Catriona Newington, used here with her kind permission.

The author's reproductions of entries in Harry's pilot logbooks are taken from the Private Papers of Group Captain McClaren-Reid D.F.C. (Documents.322) by permission of the Imperial War Museum, which has made every effort to trace the copyright owners.

Images otherwise credited to 'The Author' are reproduced from photographs in his collection or, in the case of maps, drawn by the author on base maps supplied by d-maps.com.

Catriona Newington

4	Margaret Copeman	63	Harry and fellow officer, Kirkuk
11	Wedding portrait	103	Harry and cricket eleven
17	Mother and two daughters	107	Margaret, Harry and dog
21	Horace and Margaret in the snow	117	Unknown newspaper photo
22	Horace's bungalow	119	Margaret with father, Angela, Alasdair
24	Young Angela	122	Alasdair, friends and camel
32–3	Baghdad wedding	126	Quetta lunch party
36	Kurdish women at well	127	Westland Wapiti
37	Harry, his father and Sylvia	131	Peshawar pantomime photo
42	Margaret and new baby	132	Alasdair with his garage
44–5	Alwiyah club, Baghdad	133	Margaret and Alasdair, 1936

134	Bombs store at Peshawar
138	Victorious rifle team
139	Harry at Miranshah, 1936
141	Harry in stylish clothes
144–5	Margaret and aircraft
146–7	Diplomats procession, Lima
149	Margaret in wheelchair
151	Peruvian women and llama
152	Harry and fish catch
154	'Weird' railway in Ecuador
155	Quito scene, 1939
157	*Aquitania* dinner group, 1939
158	Alasdair in school uniform
160	Harry departing Peru, 1939
162	Margaret and friends, Santiago
163	Harry trying to bull-fight
167	Reed fishing boats on Lake Titicaca
169	Monastery at Huancayo
170–71	Gymnastics display at St Andrew's
180	Hector Buzo's gold mine
192–3	Santiago dinner group, 1942
222	Alasdair as young subaltern, 1948
237–9	Harry's RAF career

Author

2	Miniature medals of H.R. McLaren-Reid
5	Harry McLaren-Reid
48–9	Harry's flight at No. 6 Squadron
57	Letter from Mosul 1924
216	Foreign Office letter, 1946
226–7	The Old Mill House, 2021

Author
(from his collection)

(ii), (vi), (viii), 8, 27, 46, 66, 98, 122, 205, 220, 236

Author
(on d-maps.com base)

28	Map of Iraq
53	Map of NE Iraq
142	Map of South America

Author / General Registrar

26	Margaret and Harry's marriage certificate

Author / IWM Documents.322

57	Extract from Harry's log book
140	List of aircraft flown

London Gazette

230	19 October 1948, p. 5665

Richard Hards (via flickr)

68	Harry and crashed BF, Aden

Sikh Museum

18	Brighton Pavilion in 1915

Wellington College Archives

199	Wellington College group, 1944

AdobeStock_162313083

71	1920s dance scene

More titles from EnvelopeBooks
www.envelopebooks.co.uk

A Road to Extinction
JONATHAN LAWLEY

When Britain colonised the Andamans in 1857, the welfare of its African pygmy inhabitants was of no concern. Nine tribes died out. Dr Lawley now assesses survival prospects for the three remaining tribes and weighs up the legacy of his grandfather, who ran the colony in the early 1900s. EB2

Spy Artist Prisoner
GEORGE TOMAZIU

Artist George Tomaziu half-expected to be imprisoned and tortured for monitoring Nazi troop movements through Bucharest during the Second World War but thought that his heroism would be recognised when Socialism came to Romania in 1950. He was terribly mistaken. EB10

Postmark Africa
MICHAEL HOLMAN

Made an Amnesty Prisoner of Conscience while he was under house arrest as a student in Southern Rhodesia, the author went on to document Africa's emergence from colonialism as Africa Editor of the Financial Times. EB1

Why My Wife Had To Die
BRIAN VERITY

There is no known cure for Huntington's disease, a wasting condition that sufferers acquire from a parent. In this painful account, the author vents his rage at society, lawmakers, health services and the church for not grasping the need, as he sees it, to legalise compulsory sterilisation and assisted dying. EB9

From Bedales to the Boche
ROBERT BEST

Bedales, the progressive boarding school founded by J.H. Badley in 1893, instilled values that sustained many of its pupils through the rest of their lives. Robert Best recalls its influence on him as an enthusiastic army recruit in 1914 and, from 1916, in the Royal Flying Corps. EB3

My Modern Movement
ROBERT BEST

London's Festival of Britain in 1951 marked the belief that Modern design was visually, morally and commercially superior. Robert Best, the UK's leading lighting manufacturer, had more experience of making things than the intellectuals who sought to change public taste, and he thinks the dice were loaded. This is his memoir. EB8

A Girl's Own War
K.J. KELLY

In wartime Ireland, an Englishman and a German may have to fight to the death. But just a few months earlier, Flt. Lt. Oliver Carmichael and Baron Julius von Stulpnagel were living together in Berlin, trying to sell forged paintings. So why are they now in rundown Ballingore and how will ex-convent-girl Mary Collins and her devoted sidekick Niamh Slattery play into their hands? Hilarious Irish farce. EB17

The Hopeful Traveller
JANINA DAVID

A collection of short stories about—and told by—single women who have put the past behind them but are still looking for their anchor in the present. It includes bitter-sweet accounts of the freedoms of postwar life, of foreign travel, of the rekindling of old friendships and of the search for new ones. EB4

Fiction from EnvelopeBooks
www.envelopebooks.co.uk

Belle Nash and the Bath Soufflé
WILLIAM KEELING ESQ.
In the first volume of The Gay Street Chronicles, bachelor Belle Nash attempts to navigate bigotry and corruption in Regency Bath without compromising the nephew of Immanuel Kant or the legal talents of Gaia Champion. BB1

The Train House on Lobengula Street
FATIMA KARA
An anguished but life-affirming novel, set within the Indian community in Bulawayo in Rhodesia of the 1950s and 1960s, about the capacity of women to gain the same advantages as men in the modern world while remaining faithful to traditional Muslim values. Affectionate and passionate. EB12

A Sin of Omission
MARGUERITE POLAND
An emotionally intense novel, set in 1870s South Africa at a time of rising anti-colonial resistance. The book examines the tragedy of a promising black preacher, hand-picked for training in England as a missionary, only to be neglected by the Church he loves. Winner of the 2021 Sunday Times CNA 'Book of the Year' Award in South Africa. EB6

Mustard Seed Itinerary
ROBERT MULLEN
When Po Cheng falls into a dream, he finds himself on the road to the imperial Chinese capital. Once there he rises to the heights of the civil service before discovering that there are snakes as well as ladders. Carrollian satire at its best. EB5

Frances Creighton: Found and Lost
KIRBY PORTER

Love demands trust but trust is a lot to ask for victims of abuse. Having been bullied by two teachers in Belfast as a boy, Michael Roberts suppresses his childhood pains until the death of a girlfriend years later forces him to revisit lost memories. EB7

Belle Nash and the Bath Circus
WILLIAM KEELING ESQ.

In Volume Two of The Gay Street Chronicles, bachelor Belle Nash returns to Regency Bath from Grenada, inspired by a new love that leads him into various pretences that may compromise the ambitions of black circus impresario Pablo Fanque. BB2

Lagos, Life and Sexual Distraction
TUNDE OSOSANYA

Twelve short stories, mostly focused on the struggle to survive in Lagos, Nigeria's commercial capital, illustrating the tensions that exist between the generations, between the sexes and between the country's different social classes and ethnicities. The first story is set in northern Nigeria, against a background of radical religious insurgency. EB13

The Attraction of Cuba
CHRIS HILTON

Chris Hilton went to Cuba to escape the boredom of everyday life and to make money, only to be entranced by the beauty of the country and of Yamilia, a street girl who brought meaning to his life but who could not help him from falling into an inevitable downward spiral. EB14